Ronan McMahon's

PROFIT PRINCIPLE

An Insider's Guide to Doubling Your Money in Real Estate Overseas

www.InternationalLiving.com

Ronan McMahon's Profit Principle: An Insider's Guide to Doubling Your Money in Real Estate Overseas

Author: Ronan McMahon

Editor: Erica Mills

Cover photo: ©iStockphoto.com/matthewleesdixon

ISBN: 978-1-911260-16-5 120B003437

TABLE OF CONTENTS

INTRODUCTION

My name is Ronan McMahon. I'm a global real estate scout and investor. I've been hunting down and investing in real estate deals for the best part of two decades.

In this book, I'll give you my pick of the seven locations on my beat right now where I'm confident you could double your money in just five years. I'll give you the lowdown on how to play the real estate markets in those places, why they're worth your attention; and what kind of investment is likely to be the most profitable in each.

I first came to real estate investing after graduating from college. I was young, keen, and ready to profit from buying well in international real estate. Since then, I've invested numerous times all over the world. And, I've traveled extensively to find, research, and negotiate for bigger and better deals. I've visited, researched, recommended, and/or spent my own money in upward of 127 locales since I founded *Real Estate Trend Alert* in 2008. I spend more than half a million dollars a year on travel, research, and expenses related to pinpointing my best deals and putting together my reports on the stand-out opportunities.

Over the years, I've amassed a wealth of real estate knowledge, insight, and experience. The kind of experience that allows me and members of *Real Estate Trend Alert* (a real estate alert service available to a savvy group of investors) to make big profits on international real estate. This is the first time I've put all that intelligence into a single resource—and through it, I'm giving you the know-how and the strategies you'll need to do well on your own international real estate investments.

There wasn't a resource like this when I was starting out. I wish there had been. Some of the lessons that you'll learn in this book I learned the hard way. Having a resource like this at hand would have cut the time, effort, and money it cost me to become the experienced investor I am today.

Whether you're a complete beginner or an investor with some real estate experience under your belt, this book will help you to refine your investment style to suit your budget and goals.

I'll also give you the nuts-and-bolts details you need to make sound real estate investments. Knowing how to buy well is not as simple as finding a great location. It's about making sure you cut the best possible deal. That includes safeguarding yourself from any potential pitfalls.

Thanks to my tips, you'll be able to avoid the most common traps and pitfalls of international real estate investing.

Using this book as a resource, you won't have to:

- Make the costly trial-and-error mistakes beginner (and sometimes experienced) real estate investors make.
- Spend your valuable time researching the dos and don'ts of investing in real estate, both at home and abroad.
- Take endless trips overseas to track down and identify the best places in the world today to buy low and profit.
- Be blindsided by investment scams that can catch unsuspecting investors.

What you learn in this book could change the way you think about investing and give you the tools you need to maximize your profit—to double your money in some of the most desirable destinations the world has to offer.

My goal is to share with you the knowledge and insights I have spent years accumulating—to give you the tools you need to buy right the first time, every time.

Before you consider spending a penny on international real estate, you need to read this book. The information here could make…or save you…hundreds of thousands of dollars.

Wishing you good real estate investing,

Ronan McMahon

Real Estate Trend Alert

CHAPTER 1:

Put Your Money Where Your Mouth Is: A Track Record of Profitable Real Estate Deals

It's easy to do well in real estate (at least in the short term) when a market is going through a buying frenzy. You get in somewhere at the start of the frenzy, buy low, and then flip your buy soon after to another buyer, one who's likely financing his deal on cheap credit. If you get caught up in one of those frenzies, it can seem like the good times will never end. Until they do—blindsiding buyers and sending the market into a tailspin.

Fifteen years ago, you may have noted, as I did, just how many real estate "gurus" popped up when the housing market in North America and Europe was entering a boom. It seemed like anyone with even the most basic knowledge of real estate was peddling their "insights." Self-proclaimed property experts, all claiming to know the secrets of doing well in real estate, were a dime a dozen.

For a while, their claims seemed to hold water. Making a profit on real estate was like shooting fish in a barrel. You just had to buy, hold for a short time, and watch the value of your property rise. Then values became silly-expensive. The hype and the merchants of hype kept things going a little longer.

Those self-proclaimed gurus should have seen that the situation was too good to last. But they didn't. Whether through ignorance or recklessness, they continued to fuel the buying frenzy right up until the crash. You didn't have to be an expert to see it just didn't make sense. Ordinary homes were selling for 10 times' median earnings.

What happened when the crash started to gather speed in spectacular fashion in 2006, all the way up to 2012? Many of those so-called gurus fell by the wayside. When faced with a true crisis market, they didn't know how to act or to spot opportunity.

Me, I've earned my stripes the hard way. My expertise comes from countless hours of research. From putting boots on the ground all over the world to find the most attractive real estate deals. And from a track record that's more than a decade long.

I started my *Real Estate Trend Alert* service—a service that is designed to scout out opportunities for members to buy low and profit on undervalued real estate—in 2008, in the thick of the real estate crisis in the U.S. and Europe. But while other experts floundered in the crisis, *Real Estate Trend Alert* went from strength to strength. While other real estate gurus were struggling to stay afloat, *Real Estate Trend Alert* continued to grow. As did the number of members who were buying well and profiting on my recommendations.

How have I done it? There's no magic trick. It takes countless hours of research...long, often uncomfortable travel to check out new locations...strategic thinking...and a strong knowledge of different real estate markets. When the world is your beat, there's always opportunity somewhere.

And, just as important as knowing when to get in on an up-and-coming real estate locale is knowing when to get out. A market frenzy—like the one the U.S. saw up to 2006—is easy to get caught up in; it takes foresight and a good sense of timing to avoid getting caught at the height of a frenzy. That sort of frenzy can work well for us as real estate buyers—*if* we get in at the start of the growth trajectory. That means getting in before prices take off—and locking down quality real estate at low prices before it appreciates in value.

Take, for example, one of the earliest deals I made in Panama. I got in when the market was at the start of an upward growth trajectory. I bought with just $5,000 down. I pocketed $73,000 by buying a preconstruction condo for $147,000 and selling shortly after delivery for $220,000.

But while other real estate gurus might have been tempted to throw their weight behind a market like Panama and continue recommending opportunity after opportunity, I watched the market closely. Shortly after, I recognized that the opportunity had passed.

From then, I didn't make another recommendation for Panama until January 2016.

I don't tell you this to be boastful or to insult other real estate experts. It's not for the sake of ego or to impress you. That would be a waste of my time and yours—time that could be better spent researching or digging deeper into a potential opportunity. The reason I'm telling you this...and about my track record...is that it's important for you to know as a real estate investor. A real estate deal is only as good as the developer and the circumstances behind it. And a real estate expert is only as good as his track record and reputation.

In my time at *Real Estate Trend Alert* and before that, I've seen other real estate "experts" come and go—sometimes they were fly-by-night speculators who had no business advising others where to put their hard-earned dollars.

For any real estate opportunity that I recommend to my readers, I recommend they do their own due diligence. And I recommend you do the same before trusting anyone who calls him/herself an expert. If you can't find details of their track record, if they're not open and transparent about how their recommendations have performed, run the other way.

Over the years since I made my first Panama buy, I have continued to do well. That's because I look for very specific windows of opportunity in a market. I look for moments when a market is at the start of an upward growth trajectory—or pockets of opportunity where a market is set to take off.

In two years alone, I traveled to more than 25 countries on four continents, spending as much as five solid weeks on the road at a time. Each year, my time on the road increases. These days, I spend more time away than I do at home. That's all in the service of finding good deals.

To be clear, much of that travel and research comes to nothing. For every opportunity I recommend, there are 10 more that don't make the cut. Sometimes it's because the numbers don't add up...or that a market that looked promising turns out to be less exciting when I've put boots on the ground.

But none of that travel or research is wasted. After more than a decade investigating international real estate markets, I have a black book of contacts, containing the names of and direct lines to the highest-level decision makers, developers, and builders in the world, which is thicker than that of anyone I know.

In the interest of transparency and recounting my track record to you, here's how some of my recommendations have shaken out:

Brazil

In 2008, I locked down two luxury condos in a beach community in Northeastern Brazil for 180,000 Brazilian *reais* each. I was able to secure that condo with a small down payment of 1% of the condo's value—the equivalent of just $736. I paid small monthly payments of 1%.

The condo was in a prime area, came from a proven developer, and I was confident that it would appreciate in value. The rest of the world—particularly North America and Europe—was hitting crisis, but Brazil was booming. The weekend I bought my condo, the entire condo community sold out. In a matter months, before a shovel had broken ground, a buyer offered me 250,000 Brazilian *reais*. I sold, for a gross profit of $43,500. And I later sold again, while construction was still in progress on my second condo, for an even bigger gain.

A couple of months ago when I made a follow up visit I saw one of these condos listed for 550,000 *reais*. That's more than three times what I, and members of my *Real Estate Trend Alert* group, got in at in 2008.

Those were just two of my buys in Northeastern Brazil. In total, I bought six condos in the same area—before selling each at a profit.

The most recent one I sold, I bought for 200,000 *reais*. That condo grossed me 450,000 *reais* as part of a recent land deal. Over the past year, I've been investing in raw land for residential and commercial development in Northeastern Brazil.

Mexico

Mexico has proven to be an exceptional market for real estate deals in the past three years—both in the Riviera Maya, on the country's Caribbean coast, and in luxury Cabo, on the Pacific coast.

The Riviera Maya has all the things I look out for: a location that's on the up…limited potential for development…low pricing that's set to rise…and a strong rental market.

I first visited one project when it was in the early stages—about to start construction.

I was there to scout out the opportunity for members of my *Real Estate Trend Alert* (*RETA*) group. I've visited again and again and made some recommendations that have risen sharply in value.

Back when I first visited this development, real estate in this community was at bargain-level pricing. The townhome I recommended to readers of *Real Estate Trend Alert* in January 2014—I locked one down, too—was available to them for $215,000. Now it lists for almost $290,000.

In 2014, I also locked down another recommendation I'd made to *RETA* members—two loft-style condos close to the hippy-chic town of Tulúm. These lofts were launched to *RETA* members with exclusive pricing from $141,500 in February 2014. Less than 18 months later, they were listing in the $180,000s range: a massive gain in a short time. And I expect to rent those properties out in the future. In peak season, one would easily rent for up to $1,000 a week gross (before taxes and other costs).

Another deal I recommended was a small number of condos in the laidback city of Playa del Carmen. They're just blocks from the beach. When I recommended them in 2013, members of *Real Estate Trend Alert* could buy for exclusive, members-only pricing of $136,500. Today, one of those condos would list for $200,000. A paper gain of $63,500. You could comfortably rent one of those condos for $20,000 or more a year

It's not just in the Riviera Maya where I and members of my group have seen success. In high-end Cabo, the results have been as positive.

In December 2014, I made a recommendation for one of the strongest luxury deals to ever cross my desk—a chance to own a luxury condo in a golf and resort community.

The deal was to buy a luxury ocean-view condo, pre-construction, with a members-only price from $324,720. Again, I locked one down. (I never recommend anything to readers that I wouldn't be comfortable owning, too.)

When I recommended these condos, I made a bold prediction: that by the time the condo was delivered, it would list for north of $500,000. At the time of writing, the condos have just recently been delivered—and already they're well on track to hit that target. Condos like this now list in the $450,000 range.

Their rental potential is strong, too. These are true luxury—and the vacationers who will be willing to rent one are happy to pay a premium for the high-class surrounds and finishes. Within a couple of years of taking possession, I expect this condo will throw off an annual income in the region of $46,625.

Europe

People who followed my recommendations in Europe have done well in recent years. Europe, like the U.S., was hard hit by the global financial crisis...and real estate prices plummeted in some of the most attractive countries on that continent.

Despite that, not every European country in crisis was worth buying in. I kept a close eye on the situation throughout Europe and found some killer deals, especially in Ireland, Spain, and Portugal. But in other crisis-hit countries, like Greece and Italy, the opportunities didn't stack up. I made few recommendations in Italy, and none in Greece. To recommend a real estate buy, I have to see clearly a capital appreciation or strong rental income angle. I saw neither in Greece or Italy. I'm holding off making a recommendation—if any—in either of these countries until the numbers stack up. If they don't, I won't make any. It's not enough for real estate to be cheap to get a recommendation from me. There has to be a strong and clear upside in buying for me to make a recommendation.

In Ireland, Spain, and Portugal, however, the numbers *did* stack up—and stacked up well.

Strong Capital Appreciation and Rental Yields in Ireland: In 2011, I recommended buying condos in Dublin near the International Financial Services Centre (IFSC). At that point, they were selling from €140,000, well below their true value. That pricing reflected the crisis in Ireland's real estate market. In 2017, you could sell one of those condos for double that, €280,000. That's a gain of €140,000 in six years.

And you could have banked an additional €100,800 over six years in rental income along the way, for a total cash windfall of €240,800.

Crisis Opportunity in Spain: Those who followed my recommendations in the Costa del Sol saw big gains quickly. In 2014, I recommended condos in an established community on Spain's Costa del Sol for €150,000. I said that now was the time to act, as this market was set for a rebound. I was right. Now, a couple of blocks away from that community, a major U.K. developer is selling pre-construction, two-bedroom condos. The price: starting in the €400,000 range and up.

Another condo (a penthouse) I recommended in a private community, less than 10 minutes from the hip town of Puerto Banús, was priced at €129,000. Almost three years later, that penthouse would list for €259,000.

In late 2013 I recommended condos in an elegant residential community when they were selling from €95,800. Or you could pick up a penthouse for €109,900. Today one of those penthouses lists for €171,000—a gain of €61,100 in less than four years.

That's just a small handful of the opportunities I've found in Spain—but far from the only ones to see strong capital appreciation.

Real-Life Investor Examples

I'm not the only one who's done well on the opportunities I've found. Members of my *Real Estate Trend Alert* group get in contact regularly to tell me about the kinds of capital appreciation they've seen on opportunities I've brought to them.

One investor wrote in to tell me about a lot he'd bought in Corozal, Belize. He purchased the lot in 2006 for $50,000. When he sold it again in 2010, he sold it for $129,000. That's a gain of $79,000—more than double his original investment—in just four years.

Another couple acted on a recommendation I made for a property in Mexico's Riviera Maya, one of the strongest locales on my beat. They locked down a home there when pricing was at $359,000. Two years later, when they sold, that property netted them $480,000—a gain of more than $120,000.

One investor bought one of the pre-construction condos I recommended in Brazil—the same ones I invested in—in 2008. He held onto his condos until 2014. When he sold, he more than doubled his investment, turning a 215,000 *reais* condo into a 450,000 *reais* condo.

Those are all examples of how well investors can do when they know how to buy real estate. At any moment in time, there is opportunity to buy well somewhere in the world. The chapters to follow will tell you exactly how you could do it, too.

CHAPTER 2:

Why International Real Estate Can Be Insurance With Huge Upside

The investors in Chapter 1 made big profits on real estate. Making a profit is a good reason to invest in property and do it right.

But it's far from the only reason to invest in real estate overseas. Especially if you're conservative by nature. With the right real estate buys overseas, you can stay diversified while seeing huge upside with your investment.

If you're a conservative investor (or even if you're not), one of the biggest advantages to investing overseas is that you're not leaving your entire nest egg at the mercy of one market. If things were ever to go belly up in the U.S., having some of your money outside the U.S. could be the only thing to save your hide.

After a turbulent decade for the U.S. economy, the U.S. dollar is once again strong. The economy is on the up and many Americans are seeing recovery after years of challenging times. Real estate values in many locales in the States have bounced back and the stock market has rebounded. Many of the people who were looking overseas for opportunity have stopped exploring their options to invest abroad. It's human nature: When times are good, there's a temptation to be insular, and to focus on the opportunities that are closest to us. When we're happy and things are relatively good, we imagine that things will always be this good.

Understandable as that feeling is, it's short-sighted. And it can set you up for a fall if or when things aren't so great in the future.

Smart investors know the value of diversification—even when times are good. They know that to protect and grow wealth, you can't put all your eggs in one basket. Having a strong stable of foreign real estate in your portfolio can help to insulate you against market changes. When you focus your investing in one location, you're at the mercy of that market. The value of your investment rises and falls as the market changes, or as currency exchange rates weaken or strengthen.

If there's one thing you learn as a global real estate investor, it's that booms and busts are cyclical. Economies and currencies rise, and they fall again. Knowing that, it always makes good sense to diversify your portfolio—not merely across stocks, but across currencies and assets as well. That way, if you take a hit on one, life goes on.

The problem with a lot of investment portfolios is that they're closely tied to the investor's home economy and currency. That's not so bad when an economy or currency is strong. But when things aren't so good, you'll quickly see the effects of having all your investment eggs in one basket.

Your retirement account is likely to be almost 100% allocated to U.S. and dollar-denominated assets. That's a bet that the U.S. will continue unchallenged for our lifetime and beyond. As all of us saw after the last financial crisis, that's not a smart bet to make. If there's a big problem at home, your portfolio is going to take a pounding, maybe with no chance of recovery. That's why it's prudent to look beyond your home borders.

Now, my beat is, of course, real estate overseas—where, I'm pleased to report, the news is positive these days. That's not because every destination overseas is in a good place economically. As I said, economies rise and economies fall. But because I follow a well-worn strategy of pinpointing destinations on the up...where values are set to rise...my readers are able to own in locations where they're primed to make strong gains as the market appreciates. That means buying in locales where values are set to rise, thanks to a new middle and upper-middle class; where new roads, bridges or flight routes are opening up an area; or where a crisis allows you to buy for cents on the dollar.

For every opportunity I recommend, I usually recommend holding for a minimum of five to seven years—long enough to lock in the gains of capital appreciation, but not so long or short a period that you're at the mercy of market and currency changes. And I recommend owning across different locations. That insulates you from the risk that, if one market changes drastically, your entire portfolio suffers.

Follow the advice in this book, and diversification comes as the cherry on top of banking some nice profits. This isn't like putting your money in a bank overseas with a tiny annual rate of return. Buying and holding like this means that your money is naturally diversified outside the United States...while you're banking some big upsides along the way.

Using Real Estate as "Insurance" Against a Downturn

You can use overseas real estate as a hedge against bad times at home. It's like "insurance." Unlike traditional "insurance," using overseas real estate as a hedge isn't "dead money" if nothing bad actually happens. In fact, it has a whole lot of upside—regardless of the state of the economy back home.

Let me give you an example: In April 2008, I stood on a hill overlooking a stretch of white-sand beach, one of the finest in all of Brazil. From where I was standing, it was easy to forget about what was happening back home. It was serene. The peaceful sound of the waves lapping the shore was a far cry from the turmoil many investors were dealing with then in the U.S. and Europe, where real estate markets had stalled. Those real estate markets quivered on the precipice of a massive collapse.

But in Northeast Brazil, things were different. No one was panic selling. They had no reason to. At that moment in time, the economy was looking good for Brazil. A new middle class was emerging. And I'd been watching with satisfaction how the market was growing. In fact, far from panic selling, the locals were panic *buying*. That new middle class had money to spend on real estate. And they were afraid if they didn't act soon, they'd miss their opportunity to buy a new and shiny condo in one of the hottest developments. Put simply, the real estate market in Northeast Brazil was on a tear, thanks to a fast-growing domestic economy.

I was on that hill to see a new condo release in action. And at that event, properties were selling out fast. In this case, I was one of the lucky ones able to lock down a couple of condos early, thanks to a special pre-release deal I'd negotiated—the rest were all but sold out within a day.

Values immediately rose and continued to rise throughout the crisis in the U.S. and Europe. Plus, the value of the currency rose as well, adding to the gains I had already locked in. I bought more condos in this part of Brazil, and their values, too, continued to soar through the 2009 real estate crash in the U.S., Europe, and beyond. There was strong demand from long-term renters, too.

Right now, the economy in Brazil is different. There's crisis playing out there as I write—with uncertainty in the country's political system, and with the economy in much of the country taking a nose dive. The currency is weaker now, too. But my investments in 2008 were still strong ones. I took advantage of the right buying moment—and doing so insulated me against the problems other investors in the U.S. and Europe were facing.

In other words: My investments in Brazil moved in exactly the opposite direction to real estate values and the stock market back home.

Even now, despite the problems Brazil is dealing with economically and politically, those condos—if you'd bought when I recommended—would remain a good buy. Tenants are still sending their rent checks every month and owners have still locked in gains from capital appreciation.

The Ultimate Insurance Policy

A condo buy can be a good investment (assuming you've bought the right type of property in the right place). But if you want to be well diversified, you shouldn't just rely on one type of property buy, such as residential homes. By thinking outside the box, you could further diversify your real estate portfolio.

One way to do that is by owning farmland. It's one of the simplest but best ways I know to own a type of property that will always be in demand.

People will always have to eat. That's just a fact of life. That's why I think of farmland as the ultimate insurance policy. No matter what happens, there will always be demand for food, regardless of the value of the dollar or of your portfolio. The world's population is booming—and productive farmland is a valuable commodity. And, as the global population continues to grow, the value of good quality agricultural land will only increase. (I'll tell you more about productive farmland in Chapter 12.)

Diversity of Demand in Internationalized Tourist Hot-spots

In some of the tourist hot-spots I recommend, you could make a killing on rental income. By choosing a location with international demand, you insulate yourself against losses, should one type of vacationer stop coming. When you have demand from all over the world, should one particular market segment dry up, you're not exposed to the risk of all your rental income drying up.

Take, for example, Mexico's Riviera Maya. It's a location that's seriously on the up. This is a boom location, thanks to Mexico's fast-growing economy and the Riviera Maya's attractiveness. Demographic changes north of the border are helping fuel demand. More North American retirees and Mexican diaspora are looking to live here. The retirees come to escape rising costs back home, for personal or political reasons, or just because they want a home in the sun.

Vacation numbers are strong from the U.S. and Canada, too. Right now, demand is strong from North American vacationers and expats. But the opportunity to do well on real estate on the Riviera Maya doesn't rely solely on that demand. The rental properties that my *RETA* members have been buying here are in strong demand from the European and Latin American markets—and even Australians and New Zealanders. If Americans stopped coming, there would still be renters. Maybe not as many as before, but enough to still see a healthy rental income.

Take Spain and Portugal, for example. Both countries get heavy tourist numbers—particularly from the rest of Europe. In the wake of Brexit, there's been some speculation that British citizens will stop coming. If travel within the EU is restricted, it could be more difficult for people from the UK—particularly retirees—to emigrate. They may not be allowed to bring their government pensions (the equivalent of Social Security in the U.S.) as they have done until now.

It could have an effect on the real estate market in Europe. But it won't be devastating for Spain or Portugal. Tourists and expats from Ireland, Scandinavia, Germany, and elsewhere will still come. By buying in a place with international demand—one that doesn't just rely on one type of vacationer or nationality—you're better positioned to absorb changes in a market.

Diversification Against Changes to the Dollar

As I write this, the dollar is in a good place. The international shock of Brexit (the vote by the British to exit the European Union) has been felt across the world. After Brexit, the pound sterling, Britain's currency, fell to a 31-year low. The U.S. dollar surged in value immediately after the news of the results.

But currencies are precarious. If the last decade has taught us anything, it's that nothing is certain when it comes to global currencies. Just because a currency is strong today doesn't mean it will be in years—or even months or days—to come.

If your portfolio is entirely reliant on one single currency's staying strong, you could be in for a shock if things take a turn for the worst. If you have an entirely dollar-denominated, stock-heavy retirement portfolio, you're exposing yourself to two big risks: inflation and currency devaluation. Both of these can erode your buying power and force you to dip into your savings sooner and more often than you'd planned.

Diversification—across asset classes, across markets, and across currencies—is a way to hedge that risk. By investing in real estate markets that don't use the dollar, you minimize your risk and have greater potential to maximize your returns.

Currency is a key consideration in real estate purchases in many locales on my beat. In places like Brazil, Spain, Ireland, Colombia, and Thailand, real estate is priced in the local currency. Right now your dollar buys you more local currency than it did a year ago. Your dollars are now worth more in international real estate terms than they were in the past.

So if you want to lock in some of this strength—or hedge against a weaker dollar in the future—you can do this through international real estate, while also getting exposure to stronger growth trends than exist back home.

For example, in Northeast Brazil my recommendation is to buy the real estate that Northeast Brazil's new middle and upper-middle class will want to own. Northeast Brazil makes, or manages the export of, commodities that the world needs: shoes, petro chemicals, watermelons, gas, oil. Despite some of the issues the rest of Brazil is facing economically and politically, in Northeast Brazil, business is brisk and employment is strong. Your tenant in Brazil will still be able to send a rent check even if the U.S. economy isn't strong.

It works the opposite way, too. If the U.S. economy—and as a result, the dollar—is strong, your money can stretch further overseas.

That's something members of my *Real Estate Trend Alert* group have taken advantage of in Europe. In the past three years, the dollar has strengthened hugely against the euro. At the height of the dollar's strength, it was stretching 25% more than it had just a year previously against the euro. That meant your budget could have bought you a lot more than it had just a year earlier.

If you'd got in at the height of the dollar's strength, you could have snapped up something at bargain pricing. Then, when the currencies' strengths were reversed—with the euro strong against the dollar—you'd have locked in more gains when you went to sell to a European buyer.

CHAPTER 3:

Location # 1: Where You Could Potentially Double Your Money in 5 Years—Mexico's Riviera Maya

Now we get to the fun stuff: the first of seven locations where I'm confident you could double your money in five years.

But I should probably answer a question first: How do you find a place where you can double your money in five years? That's a tricky one to answer. (Especially given that most of this book deals with that question.) But I'll try to give you the long and short of it.

Short answer: Doing well in real estate has a lot to do with timing. Get in at the right point of a growth trajectory, or buy when a market is in crisis but set for a resurgence, and you could stand to make a killing when real estate values rise.

That explanation may make it sound easy. But in reality, finding that right buying moment is tricky.

Here's the longer answer: You have to know the markets you want to buy in. You have to do your research—a lot of it. Last year alone, my team and I racked up tens of thousands of dollars and countless hours in research and scouting trips.

Before I—or any of my team—scout, we research heavily to identify possible buying moments in a market. Then we put boots on the ground to check out the opportunity in person. I've visited hundreds of different locations in the past decade to investigate them further. Some that looked good on paper didn't stack up in reality. I only recommend a tiny proportion of the properties I scout—and only the very best deals.

Once we've put boots on the ground, the research isn't over. We pore over the paperwork. Do the calculations. Run through the legalese with a fine-tooth comb. And then double- and triple-check the facts. If one thing doesn't add up or the deal isn't working out as initially promised, that's it. I'll pull the plug. I don't recommend anything I won't stand behind 100%—or anything I wouldn't personally invest in. I'm extremely selective in what I recommend. I have to be. My reputation relies on only telling my readers about the best deals out there.

That said, that level of research is not just something I do. If you're investing or planning to invest in real estate, it's something that you should do as a matter of course, too. You need to know, down to the tiniest detail, what you're buying—and what makes it a good buy.

If you do it right, you stand to make a killing. Because when everything stacks up on the right deal, you could see your profit soar. All the deals I've recommended in my time have significant upside—whether that is through capital appreciation, strong rental yields, or a mixture of both.

The gains aren't small when you do it right. In the seven destinations I'll tell you about in this book, you could stand to double your money in just five years.

A Day in the Life of a Real Estate Scout

It's not every day you find yourself standing in the middle of a thicket of jungle with a man holding a machete. For most people, that would be your cue to run a mile.

But for me, it's all in a day's work. Trekking to off-the-beaten-path stretches of paradise is how I find the best up-and-coming deals and locations.

As my companion, Carlos, raised his machete to slice through the scrub, I took a deep breath, filling my lungs with the warm, clean, Caribbean air. A brightly colored butterfly flitted by my face.

With a few flicks of his wrist, Carlos had cleared a path for us. He motioned ahead of us with the machete.

"We're nearly there."

Carlos stands around five feet tall, a tiny figure beside my six-foot-something frame. But in the boardroom, he cuts a big figure. He's one of the Riviera Maya's most successful developers, spending a lot of his time flying first-class to Mexico City or running the rule over plans and projects.

He's in his element here, though, on Mexico's Riviera Maya (the name given to the Caribbean coast running from Cancún to Tulúm), tramping through the jungle.

He'd brought me here to show me the site for a new project. He was very excited.

"I can't to wait show you this…," he told me with a wide smile. That smile is contagious. I couldn't help but grin back at him.

With a flourish, Carlos flicked his machete three more times and the path was finally cleared. As I stepped behind him, I could see why he'd been so excited to lead me here. In front of us, the most spectacular *cenote* (sinkhole) I have ever seen opened up in front of us like a giant amphitheater.

Overhead, tropical birds called and swooped from tree to tree.

Our journey of discovery wasn't over yet. Carlos motioned for me to follow, and we walked along the edge of the cenote. He hacked again at some scrub to clear my view and then pointed down. I peered down at where he pointed: A hole in the ground—another cenote—no wider than three feet but perfectly symmetrical. The hole drops directly down to a white-bottomed underground lake and cavern. It's beautiful and peaceful.

This is where Carlos had chosen to build a project, one of the best I've found on the Riviera Maya. The cenotes are still there. (They're protected by law so they can't be built on.)

And the development here complements the Caribbean landscape. There are no concrete monstrosities or looming condo towers. Everything is low-rise and low-density. Carlos appreciates what makes the Riviera Maya such a stunning place. He knew that, to keep it special, he had to preserve the raw beauty of the land. And that's what I like about the best developments on the Riviera Maya. They're not replacing the natural Caribbean beauty. Instead, they're making sure development complements the beauty here.

It makes this coast a special place. And more and more people are starting to discover it.

The Riviera Maya's Path of Progress Story

The Riviera Maya wasn't always the vacation paradise it is today. In fact, up until a few decades ago, it was completely off most travelers' radar. Thanks to some heavy investment, it's emerging as one of the world's best tourist destinations.

Mexico is serious about tourism. Fonatur is the most successful tourism promotion body on earth. There was a time when no one had heard of Cancún or the Riviera Maya. Then along came Fonatur.

Back in the late 1960s, Cancún was an almost uninhabited, sandy spit of land. Air travel was just taking off for the U.S. middle class. Fonatur homed in on Cancún as a locale with tourism potential. It backed Cancún. Not with an advertising campaign in inflight magazines and some trade shows. It did the real work—less likely to get instant attention, but vital for long-term, sustainable growth. It provided the infrastructure to facilitate the development of a major tourism industry. It knew what it had: stunning beaches and great weather. It knew what it lacked: a world-class hotelier and vacation company.

An international airport was built. Fonatur became, in effect, a master developer. It made plans and brought infrastructure to hotel and condo plots. Then international groups were invited in to develop. These were early days. A sweetener was needed to get the big names. They got tax breaks. Cancún has been a roaring success. Hotels are packed. Condo values soared.

Mexico backed Fonatur…Fonatur backed Cancún…those who backed Cancún made a killing.

Back then there were risks. This was a big idea in a new place, looking to capitalize on a North American, flight-driven vacation revolution. It could have been a complete flop. Now the concept has been proven.

I love Mexico's Riviera Maya. I visit every chance I get.

I've visited Mexico's Riviera Maya—a short 80-mile stretch of its Caribbean coast—dozens of times in the last few years. This is a place where I like to spend time. I've swum in cenotes…snorkeled with tropical fish and turtles…visited thousand-plus-year-old Maya ruins…dined in some of the best restaurants I've ever eaten in…and played many a round of golf.

The reason I visit the Mexican Riviera so often is because it's one of the strongest locations on my beat right now—both for capital appreciation opportunity and for serious short-term rental potential.

The success of this region sprang from nothing—literally. Before the Mexican government set its sights on developing Cancún into a vacation hotspot, this was an empty—but stunning—stretch of coast. Cancún was scrubby land that faced onto some of the world's best Caribbean beaches. But nobody knew it was here. That's not hyperbole. In the 1960s, Cancún had a grand total of a couple of hundred residents. The rest of the Riviera Maya was so sparsely populated that

Quintana Roo—the state that the Riviera Maya is in—didn't achieve statehood until 1974.

Thanks to heavy government investment, Cancún was developed into the thriving party town it is today. In just a couple of decades, it was transformed beyond recognition from its former self. That empty land, once a coconut plantation, is filled with resorts and hotels. Now more than 700,000 people call it home.

But there's more to the Riviera Maya than Cancún—much more. Especially for real estate investors. Cancún's been the go-to getaway for spring breakers and sun-seeking vacationers since the 1970s and 1980s. But forget that city's crowded beaches and noisy nightlife. More discerning and moneyed tourists are heading to the towns and beaches beyond. If you're in search of quiet, solitude, and untouched beauty, you'll find it farther down the highway—along the 80-mile stretch of coastline that makes up the Riviera Maya.

The Riviera Maya is on a tear. Progress has come fast and thick. What were once little fishing villages, like Playa del Carmen and Tulúm, are now hip destinations in their own right.

But it's far from overdeveloped. Every time I visit, I find another gorgeous bay I hadn't discovered on my previous trip. My most recent finds were Soliman Bay and Tankah. These deserted beaches—dotted with coconut palm trees, populated by curious iguanas and sea birds, with azure-blue water and total silence but for the roar of the surf—cannot be matched for tranquility and natural beauty.

And because of government restrictions, this area should never become overdeveloped. That's largely due to the presence of the Sian Ka'an Biosphere—a huge nature preserve just outside Tulúm—and strict regulations on building heights and density.

Mexico's Riviera Maya runs south of Cancún to Tulúm. The journey from the international airport is quick and easy. You can travel the entire Riviera Maya, from Cancún to Tulúm, in just over two hours on a modern highway. Just off that highway, you'll see signs for hotels and resorts, white-sand beaches, cenotes, ruins, and quad biking.

Put simply, this is a region that has a lot to offer vacationers… and they're coming in droves. The Mexican government is pushing to transform the Riviera Maya into the same tourism success story it's seen in Cancún. It aims to grow visitor numbers over the next decade. And it's already achieving what it set out to do. Tourist numbers on the Riviera Maya hit 4.4 million in 2014—double the number that arrived in 2005. This year, I expect visitor numbers to exceed 4.6 million.

Even before I made my first recommendation, I was paying close attention to how the Path of Progress—and the government investment—was playing out here. For a decade I've scouted this particular stretch of opportunity-rich coast. Back in 2009, I made my first "buy" recommendation in this region—in the Tulúm area on the southern tip of Mexico's Riviera Maya. My timing was perfect. Not everyone agreed.

Back then, Mexico was hated. *CNN* and *FOX* beamed images of narco violence, often without context. They didn't tell viewers that the dangers were mostly confined to border towns. (In fact, the Riviera Maya is counted as one of the safest areas in all of Mexico for tourists.) Swine flu fears ravaged Mexico's tourism industry. The situation outside Mexico was even worse for some—banks and even whole countries went bankrupt. Most real estate investors ran for cover. They weren't willing or able to dig deeper to see the real story of the Riviera Maya. The story I've come to know so well.

But the situation in Tulúm was so strong, the converging trends so unstoppable, that I knew the opportunity was too good to ignore. In fact, because of that financial turmoil back home, other investors weren't acting here. That created a clear and incredible buying moment. If you had followed my recommendations, you'd have been rewarded. Values have risen strongly since I made my first recommendations.

The opportunity on the Riviera Maya has been obvious to me since my first trip. When I visited, the Path of Progress was rolling down the coast from Cancún.

For me, then and now, the Riviera Maya was a no-brainer. It's a world away from the doom-and-gloom image of Mexico those TV stations were beaming into people's homes. The pace of life is easy and laidback, the people friendly and helpful. I've traveled the world and it's still among the most beautiful places I've been to.

And its Path of Progress story is far from over. Along with an ever-expanding number of vacationers, expats are coming to live here. The North American demographic trends mean that more and more Baby Boomers will want to live somewhere sunny, safe, affordable, convenient—and with First-World amenities south of the border.

Mexico's savvy tourism industry (powered by the best promotional institution in the world) is successfully targeting new middle classes across the globe from Brazil to Colombia, Poland to Russia. When you visit the Riviera Maya today, you'll hear accents from every corner of the world.

And Mexico has proven savvy in growing its other industries. While the sentiment in the U.S. toward Mexico was negative, Mexico was gaining the upper hand on China when it came to high-value manufacturing destined for the U.S. market. The country's a major hub for automobile production. The world's biggest construction company hails from Mexico, as well as the third-largest cement company. Food production, aeronautical equipment, electronics, and textiles are big export industries.

All this was clear to anyone who took the time to truly analyze this market. The thing was, many weren't taking that time. Their loss was a savvy real estate investor's potential gain. Today, all these positive trends are still present—and growing.

Profitable and Cool: Playa del Carmen, the Jewel in the Riviera Maya

Once upon a time, Playa del Carmen was a little fishing village. Many of its roads and streets were packed sand. But it has shed those humble roots. It's now a hip beach town where I like to spend time. The packed-sand streets and roads are now mostly paved or cobbled. It's a place for the young and cool to hang out. Many of those young people are coming on vacation. But many others are choosing to move here. Those who live here are opening up chic stores and restaurants. It has an artistic but modern vibe.

Playa del Carmen (often just called "Playa") has come a long way from those dirt-street origins. It's one of Mexico's most rapidly developing cities. In two decades, its once-tiny population grew by 10 times. It now has a population of more than 228,000.

The main street, Fifth Avenue, is a cool place to hang out in the evenings. It's completely pedestrianized—no traffic running through here at any time. Instead, in the morning you'll see joggers. In the evenings, it's thronged with people stopping to get something to eat or to shop in one of the late-opening stores.

Downtown Playa is a place where you can walk everywhere...pop in and out of the boutiques, dine in a top-class restaurant or opt for a more relaxed meal by candlelight on the beach. The restaurants and cafés serve everything from traditional Mexican to Thai food. The shops sell a mix of luxury goods, handcrafts, jewelry, and textiles.

Unlike in Cancún, you won't see faceless chain hotels or mega-malls here. The vibe is cooler, more laidback. You'll find chic boutique hotels, and small family-run stores selling ornate silver jewelry and locally produced earthenware and crafts. You can listen to live jazz over brunch at one of the beachfront restaurants, or kick back in a lounger in front of a chilled-out beach bar at sunset.

It draws vacationers from all over the world—upmarket vacationers who are looking to have fun at night and relax on the beach during the day. Tourists, and their spending power, are the big driver of the market here. For those who are regular visitors—and the city gets a lot of repeat tourists—Playa is developing and prospering right before their eyes. Each time I visit—I've lost count of how often I've visited in the past three years—Fifth Avenue has gotten longer, and more trendy restaurants and boutiques have opened up.

But the economy is not just centered on visiting tourists. Playa has become a vibrant city economy in itself. Now it's attracting more and more mobile entrepreneurs and business people.

Young entrepreneurs have moved from all over the world in recent years to open bars and restaurants, stores, and service businesses.

And Mexico's own quickly-growing middle class is increasing in numbers in Playa. They include doctors, lawyers, and engineers. Many are young professionals who started their careers in the U.S., but who are being drawn back to Mexico by the steady economic growth and trajectory.

Where I've Seen Values Double

Thanks to Playa's growing vacationer numbers and growth of middle-class professionals, this is a red-hot rental market. Short term. Long term. By the night, week, or year. You name it, you can make money from it here.

I was waiting for the right opportunity to play this market. And in June 2013, I found it. A developer had come up with a concept that would appeal to both long- and short-term renters. The idea: comfortable, luxury condos a short stroll from Fifth Avenue. On site, five-star hotel amenities were planned: including a rooftop pool and terrace, a 24-hour business center, a concierge desk, and comfortable outside spaces.

Now completed, the condos have delivered exactly what they promised. You can walk to Fifth Avenue's action in five to 10 minutes, but you're away from the sometimes noisy atmosphere of late-night revelers. You can watch a movie outdoors on comfortable, covered loungers. You can even order a babysitter if you're staying with little ones.

These condos have cross-market appeal. They combine city and beach living all in one, in a place where you could comfortably live and spend time without a car. A great little *pied-à-terre* or rental.

Back when I first recommended these condos to members of my *Real Estate Trend Alert*, they were pre-construction (also sometimes called "off plan"—see Chapter 12 for more about buying pre-construction). I had negotiated special members-only pricing of $136,500. Now one of those condos lists in the region of $200,000. That's a paper gain of $63,500.

And given the red-hot rental market, with some good marketing and a bit of effort on your part, a buyer could potentially make an impressive rental yield—around $25,000 a year gross. If you were to rent for just four years, that's a gross yield of $100,000. Couple that with the $53,500 paper gain and an early-in buyer could potentially make $153,500 in the first five years after delivery.

As Playa has continued to grow, the opportunity to buy low here and to profit has passed for the moment. But I'm keeping a close eye on this market for any similar opportunities that may arise in the future.

The Fast-Moving Tulúm Market Spells Profit

When I first visited Tulúm more than a decade ago, there wasn't much to see. At least not much in the way of development, anyway.

A friend had promised that we were going to see a piece of paradise. I trusted her instincts. She's traveled all over the world and she doesn't use a word like that lightly. So, on the back of that recommendation, I endured 90 minutes of bouncing over massive potholes and rutted, sand roads to reach this promised piece of paradise. These days, there's a modern, paved highway from Cancún's international airport to Tulúm. It's an easy, quick drive. But back then, it was a trying journey.

As we hit yet another pothole, I was beginning to wonder if the trip was going to be worth it.

When we finally came to a stop, I realized that my friend was not exaggerating. The white sand beach was completely deserted. We sat under a rustic *palapa* and gazed out at the turquoise waters. She had promised to bring me to a piece of paradise, and she delivered.

We had arrived in the first gasp of development in Tulúm. Tulúm a couple of decades ago was similar to 1960s Cancún. Though home to the ruins of a walled, ancient Maya city, it had largely been overlooked. Progress had rolled down the coast in the decades following Cancún's success, but Tulúm was at the end of the line.

It's beautiful here. Tulúm has Caribbean powder-sand beaches. The jungle hides ancient Maya ruins and white-bottomed lagoons. Brightly colored butterflies flutter on the breezes and lazy iguanas soak in the sun. When I first visited Tulúm, it was virgin territory.

It hasn't yet hit the beach-city status of Playa del Carmen or become as busy as either Playa or Cancún. Instead, it's a place to chill out. And that's exactly how the vacationers who come to Tulúm like it.

But even the fact that you can now call it a town tells you how much it has grown. A decade ago, it was little more than a village with a bohemian vibe. Go back further and its bohemian origins are even more transparent: Thirty-five years ago, when *International Living*'s writers visited Tulúm, it was home to mostly empty beaches and naked hippies.

Things have changed rapidly in Tulúm in the last decade. It still attracts a hippy crowd—backpackers and high-earning executives who still want to indulge their hippy spirit on a two-week vacation. People of all ages do yoga poses on the beach at sunrise and sunset. (They tend to be clothed these days.) There's a wide choice of organic, vegan, and vegetarian eateries.

But Tulúm has gone mainstream in a big way. It's becoming jet-set. The "feel" of Tulúm is still rustic chic. Yet this is a place where celebrities come for a yoga retreat.

Actors and models hang out in luxurious resorts. Demi Moore, Reese Witherspoon, Orlando Bloom, Cameron Diaz, and Jared Leto have all been spotted here. Stay on the beach and it will cost you. A little cabana on the beach can easily set you back between $200 and $300 a night…and places book up months in advance. One beach hut I inquired about had a price of $1,200 a night.

You can find hostels and places on a budget here; but one contact, booking months in advance, could not find a basic but comfortable hotel for under $120 a night in December. She ended up giving glamping (glamorous camping) a go—and paid $180 in total for three nights… before taxes and charges. She reports that it was fun but inconvenient. As the glamping site was on the edge of town, her walk into town was 20 minutes. The beaches were at least a 45-minute walk away. That's the level of demand in Tulúm in high season.

Here, demand far exceeds supply for rental condos. Rates regularly run to $250 and more per night. The shortage of rentals isn't just in peak season, but right through the year—and right along the coast from Tulúm to Playa del Carmen.

The appeal isn't because of Tulúm Town itself. (The name Tulúm refers to the town, the Maya ruins, and Tulúm Beach.) The town itself isn't particularly pretty by tourist standards. But even here you can see the signs of progress. Only eight years ago, the town had one supermarket, no banks and no decent eateries. Today, it's got several banks, some nice restaurants and cafés, a new gourmet supermarket, and a buzzing nightlife scene.

But the real appeal of Tulúm is just outside town, on the beach. That's where the rich and famous hang out—and where you'll find boutique (read: high price) hotels…bike rental shops and yoga classes on the beach…and some of the best restaurants I've ever eaten in.

The Hartwood restaurant, for example, is a foodie darling. It's racking up column inches in travel magazines and newspapers' food pages. In keeping with Tulúm's "natural" vibe, everything is done by hand in Hartwood. People line up for hours just to get a table. It opens at 5 p.m. But when I was there earlier this year, a long line was already winding its way along the road—at 2.15 p.m. The East Coast hipsters who stood waiting in retro hats and intentionally mismatched bikinis were content to wait hours to get in.

But even though Tulúm has gone somewhat mainstream, real estate prices have yet to catch up—at least in certain pockets of opportunity. The nearby Sian Ka'an biosphere is a protected, UNESCO World Heritage site, and strict controls on building height and density mean that development should stay restricted in much of the Tulúm area.

When I found opportunity to buy only 15 minutes' drive from the town of Tulúm, I knew it was time to act.

Two Killer Opportunities: One Developer

Along the modern highway that leads to Tulúm—five minutes past one of the most popular snorkeling locations for tourists on this coast—a grand stone arch sits on the right-hand side. It's the entrance to the residential side of a five-star, all-inclusive resort.

Within the resort, there's a 27-hole golf course. A shuttle brings you to a white-sand beach where protected turtles nest. Grand, Botero-inspired sculptures sit at the end of paved roads. The grounds are landscaped—but farther back is untouched jungle where you'll see tropical birds and butterflies…and sometimes even a coati or wild deer.

The resort has everything a traveler might want: a gym, spa, restaurants, bars, cafés, a market, and evening entertainment.

Within this resort is where I've found some killer deals. Besides the onsite hotels, the resort is also home to new residential communities. Not all of them are a buy: But some stand out as "no-brainer" deals.

Some of the best opportunities I've found here come from the same developer as in Playa del Carmen. One of the opportunities was to own a townhome. I locked one down in January 2014, when they were selling to members of my *Real Estate Trend Alert* group for $215,000.

As of writing, my townhome is complete—and I have fully furnished it. And, in a little over two years, the list price for one of these townhomes has risen to $287,370. That's a gain of $72,370.

Once the community is built out, you could rent out one of these townhomes when you aren't using it. With the right marketing, you could easily generate $24,000 gross rental income a year while using it yourself part-time. Over five years, that's a potential gross income of $120,000. Combined with the $72,370 increase in value (and I expect this townhome to keep rising in value as the Path of Progress continues through the Riviera Maya), that's a potential gross yield on my investment of more than $190,000. Not quite double—but not far off.

It's far from the only killer deal I've found here—or the only buy I've recommended that's risen in value. Typically, the deals I've recommended in that development have risen by up to 40% in value during construction alone.

As the Riviera Maya's tourist numbers continue to grow, so too will the demand for a townhome or condo in a top-notch resort like this one.

The best way to buy in the Riviera Maya is to buy resort properties, pre-construction homes, and condos for short-term rental. You lock in gains from the beginning and, if you do it right, strong capital appreciation as your property is constructed. Once built, you can target rental income from the growing number of vacationers who come here. Do it right and you could make a strong rental yield. (See Chapter 13 for more on how to make a killer rental yield.)

Wait too long and the opportunity could pass. The time to act along this stretch of coast is now. Once mainstream prices catch up with this increasingly mainstream location, the opportunity will be gone.

But get in now and this is one location where you could stand to double your money in the next five years.

CHAPTER 4:

Location # 2: Where You Could Potentially Double Your Money in 5 Years—Northeast Brazil

Picture the scene: The beach is empty. The air is full of the sound of crashing surf. A warm breeze whistles through my fraying Panama hat. Turning left and right I can see nothing but miles of white-sand beach. The water winks invitingly. It's tempting to dash in its direction and dive into the incoming surf. A warm 86-degree sunny day like today is typical most of the year. April can be muggy and rainy ...but then again it can often be like today.

There are no kite surfers on the beach today. Maybe they are around the point, where the beach is less sheltered from the trade winds. They come here from across the globe to ride. Just offshore, with pink and yellow sails full of wind, a *jangada* races parallel to the deep and wide white-sand beach. *Jangadas* are the flat-bottomed boats local fishermen use to ply their trade and sometimes to sail and race recreationally.

Now with my back to the ocean, I see low dunes covered in grasses. Beyond that are gently sloping hills, and in the distance giant wind turbines tower over fields and dunes below.

It feels like I'm a world away from the noise and hurry of a big city. But I'm not in some remote outpost—I'm just 40 minutes west of Fortaleza, Brazil's number-one domestic tourism destination. Not the sort of place you might expect to see big real estate gains. Or to potentially double your real estate investment.

But it is. This area, and the stretch of coast where I'm standing, is set to be transformed. The beach is empty today, but over the coming decades more and more Brazilians (and some foreigners) will vacation, retire, and have second homes here.

Already, plenty of tourists come: Fortaleza is surrounded by hundreds of miles of dazzling, white-sand beaches. Its clear, tropical ocean waters maintain a year-round temperature of 80° F. Serving as the glimmering centerpiece for the state of Ceará, this capital city of almost 3 million people is the number-one tourist destination in Brazil. Fortaleza boasts its own beautiful in-city beaches, buzzing nightlife, and great restaurants.

And the growth of Fortaleza does not look set to stop any time soon.

This pocket of Northeast Brazil has been a runaway success story in the last few decades. Even at times when greater Brazil's economy has shrunk or hit speedbumps, the economy of Fortaleza has continued to grow. In Fortaleza and the area that surrounds it, you won't just find one opportunity to potentially double your investment—you'll find several, some of which I've listed in this chapter.

This is a destination I've had my eye on for the better part of a decade. I first wrote about Fortaleza, and the stretch of coast to the east and west, in *International Living* in January 2008. Back then I said:

> *"Until I discovered this region, I had become resigned to the thought that cheap and relatively accessible beachfront was a thing of the past....*
>
> *"...As far as I'm concerned, Fortaleza is the best beachfront buy on the planet right now. An opportunity like this doesn't happen often. When it does, you need to be ready to move... and to move fast.*
>
> *"...Those who get in early and buy quality stand to make a killing."*

Since then Brazil has become a middle-class economy. At the time of writing, it's going through some political turmoil and the economy and the currency are feeling the effects. But still, the story for Brazil—and especially Northeast Brazil—is strong. And there are several reasons why Brazil will remain strong, even if, right now, it's not the investor's darling it was earlier this decade. Brazil has what the world needs and wants:

- **Food:** Brazil is one of the world's largest agricultural producers, and it has vast potential to add capacity in the uncultivated grasslands of the states of Bahia and Mato Grosso. It's already a major producer and exporter of soybeans, oranges, coffee, rice, wheat, corn, sugarcane, and beef.
- **Energy:** Brazil is energy-independent. It has its own oil resources, much of which it exports. Since 1980, it has increased its total deepwater oil production almost 10 times. And that's before it starts to bring oil ashore from the recently discovered, giant Lula (formerly Tupi) field. It's one of the largest oil discoveries in the Western Hemisphere in the past 30 years.

  But Brazil is not dependent on fossil fuels. It's future-proofing itself against falling reserves, and the hit oil prices have taken, in the form of renewable energy. Almost 85% of its domestic power comes from renewable sources, around 70% from hydroelectric sources. And it's also investing heavily in solar and wind.
- **Water:** Much of Brazil sits on a giant aquifer—the world's biggest. (It shares the aquifer with Uruguay and Paraguay.) The aquifer could provide the entire world's water needs for 20 years. Brazil has the world's largest freshwater reserves. In a world where water shortages are becoming more pronounced every year, that's an important asset.
- **Minerals:** Minerals are abundant in Brazil and represent much of its top exports. Brazil's leading mineral export (and, in fact,

its leading overall export) is iron ore. That's followed by gold, niobium (a metal used in jet engines), and copper.

And with a young population and a strong manufacturing sector (Brazil makes its own planes, trains, and automobiles), Brazil has the capacity to produce larger quantities and add more value in the production process.

Today, in Northeast Brazil and in Fortaleza, there is still opportunity. Maybe more opportunity than in early 2008.

The news out of Brazil recently hasn't all been positive. The economy is in a bad state. The *real*, Brazil's currency, has been hit hard.

The political crisis has thrown the country into recession in 2015 and 2016. The effects are most pronounced in the south of the country. It's hit hardest by the recession. But this proves why digging deeper into a country can yield big results for a savvy real estate investor. While many have written off Brazil, not all of the country is suffering. In the Northeast, the economy is still growing.

Tourists are still coming and industry continues to grow.

You'd never know it from the real estate market. The economy has made real estate buyers nervous, even in the Northeast. In September 2015, the Brazilian currency dropped to a record low against the U.S. dollar. That creates more opportunity for overseas real estate buyers. Your dollar stretches further than ever before.

This is a classic "crisis investment" play—you buy while the economy is in crisis and you're sitting pretty when the economy rallies. I've seen similar crisis situations play out in Europe—in Ireland, Spain, and Portugal.

But I don't recommend buying just anything in the Northeast. The opportunity has to be right and your approach careful. Get it right and there are big profits to be made.

You need to be selective. You want to focus your search on a small number of pockets of opportunity. Or on situations where a seller wants or needs to sell up fast. And, you need to move quickly to snap up the best deals.

Driving the Opportunity to Profit: The Northeast's Hub of Industry

One of the biggest drivers of growth in the Northeast comes courtesy of a huge government program in Pecem, close to Fortaleza—the Pecem Zone for Processing of Exports (ZPE).

The announcement of this new free trade zone in May 2010 was a big deal for the Northeast.

The ZPE is a huge duty-free zone—10,500 acres—established adjacent to the Port of Pecem. Businesses located within this area will pay practically no taxes on inputs purchased...and finished goods exported.

An estimated 200 export-oriented companies are expected to set up extensive operations in this free trade zone. Many are already in full swing, including five cement factories, a wind turbine factory, and an animal feed plant. The steel factory that in June 2016 produced its first piece of steel is set to be a major employer. It's already been a massive employer before a single piece of steel goes out. The construction phase alone provided 23,000 jobs. It's gearing up for full production as I write. As it starts up, it will employ 2,800 employees directly, as well as 1,200 contractors.

The effect of this growth in industry is that many educated young people from Northeast Brazil will no longer need to move to find employment. Traditionally, once they received their degree, they moved south for work or to the U.S. or Europe. Not so now. Jobs are coming for them here and the middle class is growing in Northeast Brazil.

What's happening in Pecem is a big deal. This area is set to become a global powerhouse. Well-connected locals have been discreetly buying up everything they can in that area.

Of the hundreds of thousands of jobs that will be created, tens of thousands will be very highly skilled and highly paid. Companies are aggressively recruiting from other parts of Brazil, Europe, the U.S., and Asia. An additional 50,000 jobs are set to be created in the next five years.

There will be big opportunities to provide housing to these folks.

Already, billions of dollars have and are being invested in infrastructure to create this manufacturing and export hub next to the new world-class port.

Here's a taster of some of the projects that are going on:

- The Vale steel plant will be one of the largest in South America. It's under construction and nearing completion. The project will cost $4.8 billion (USD) and is expected to create 23,000 direct and indirect jobs.
- Studies into the expansion of the port of Pecem are well underway. Authorities plan to add a new pier on which there will be three extra docking stations (they're up to nine docking stations so far). That comes on the back of a deal between the Panama Canal Authority and Port of Pecem, which have agreed to cooperate on a new trade route, replacing the currently used Brazil-Asia route.

  That will make Pecem an even more important trade route. Pecem is the only port in the region that allows Post-Panamax ships (those too large to fit through the locks of the Panama Canal) to dock. Pecem is meeting a need that no one else is. The planned docking stations will be able to simultaneously dock and load/unload nine Post-Panamax ships.

- A planned new power plant is up and running. No sooner was it built than it was clear it wouldn't have enough capacity for the ZPE. Another is under construction.
- Within the ZPE, production of wind power turbines, cement, and fertilizers is already underway.

Own Where People Will Want to Live—Before Prices Rise

The case for Pecem is strong. And its effect on Northeast Brazil and her real estate market has been dramatic. All those highly skilled and highly paid professionals who are coming—engineers, managers, chemists, and more—will need somewhere to live. They won't want to live too close to Pecem. There's nothing appealing for a homeowner or renter there. It's an industrial zone. Instead, they'll be looking close by, to towns in close commuting distance.

Some of them will base themselves in Fortaleza. Others will be looking for a smaller beach town closer to Pecem, with all of the conveniences of Fortaleza on their doorstep.

It's not just those professional people who are creating the opportunity here. Fortaleza, as I've mentioned, is Brazil's biggest domestic tourism destination. It's a large city, stretching along more than 12 miles of coastline. Sandy beaches line the shores. It's modern and First World, thanks in part to massive investment in recent years. The government spent billions of dollars improving the city's infrastructure ahead of the 2014 soccer World Cup.

But more and more tourists are looking for something a little different. They want to have the conveniences of Fortaleza close by but to feel like they're a world away. They're seeking out smaller beach towns close to Fortaleza for their vacations, so they can have the relative quiet of relaxing on the beach, away from the traffic and noise of a city…but they can hop into Fortaleza when they want.

Wealthy folks from Fortaleza, too, are keen to escape the tourist crowds, when the city is at its busiest. They've snapped up lots and multi-million-dollar homes along the coast. Where they lead, others are following.

One of those beach towns is where a buyer who acted on one of my recommendations could have doubled his money in five years. It appeals both to the vacationer crowds and to the middle-class professionals who want to live outside of Fortaleza or close to Pecem. It's a town called Cumbuco, and it's taking off just as I predicted when I first visited eight years ago.

A Charming Beach Town Where You Could See a Big Return on Investment

I liked Cumbuco from the moment I first visited in 2008. The streets are lined with fishermen's homes. They take pride in their homes. Flowers in full bloom crawl over freshly painted exteriors. For a playground, the kids have miles of beach and a soccer ball. The beach is also their parents' "office," where they repair fishing nets and touch up the paint on their fishing boats.

For neighbors, the fishermen's homes have restaurants, a trendy kite-surfing shop, grocery stores, and beach bars where bronzed adventurers come to enjoy *caipirinhas* at sunset to the soft melodies of chill-out tracks.

It's a pretty little beach town. The perfect place to relax…as a vacationer or as an executive who wants to unwind after a hard day's work. The pace of life feels slow, but it's funky, active, and energetic. There's a buzz to the town in the evenings but not a raucous one. It's the kind of place where people are more interested in chilling out than partying hard.

It feels like some of the beach towns I've visited that are far away from modern conveniences—the sort of pristine beach town you'd expect to find way off the beaten track. But a big part of Cumbuco's appeal is its location. It's close to both Fortaleza and Pecem.

In fact, from the beach in Cumbuco, you can see the high-rises of Fortaleza in the distance. It's less than an hour's drive away. Pecem is even closer—less than 30 minutes away.

When I first visited Cumbuco in April 2008, I made a bold prediction about this sleepy little spot. I said that it was set to embark on a big upward trajectory.

I was right: This town has taken off in a big way. For folks who got in on Cumbuco in 2008, it's proven profitable.

Vacationers and second-home owners come from all over the world. More Brazilians are coming, too. This beach town is now trendy chic. Major groups have snapped up land to develop on the edge of town.

But it's not in danger of being overdeveloped. Cumbuco is low density compared to other surrounding locales. A little oasis. Down the coast, the developers have written the density laws to pack in as many condos as they wanted. Here, the wealthy folks who own homes don't want their little piece of paradise spoiled. They're working to ensure that density remains low and that Cumbuco stays just as charming and chic as it is right now.

I've found more opportunity since I first visited. Just last year, I uncovered a new opportunity to take advantage of Brazil's crisis and the drop in currency values.

Right on the edge of little Cumbuco is a master-planned resort. It was planned and developed by Vila Gale. The name may not be familiar to you, but it's one of Portugal's largest hotel groups.

Vila Gale started its development before the crisis hit. It snapped up an almost four-mile-long curve of stunning beach right on the edge of Cumbuco town. In the first phase of development, it built its own luxury hotel. It's stunning. They've gone all out to appeal to a vacationer: a spa, Turkish bath, sauna, Jacuzzi, as well as three restaurants and three bars. Guests can rent buggies to traverse the sand dunes and check out nearby lagoons.

On one of my previous trips, I was quoted $350 for a night's stay. The price wasn't discouraging anyone; it was packed to the rafters.

In the next phase of the development, the company built luxury condos that are dotted around the hotel. The vast majority of the 354 condos it built have sold.

But there are still some left—and their pricing reflects the current crisis. If you had asked me what one of these condos was worth in 2012, my best guess would have been that these condos were heading for a 400,000 *reais* launch price as part of a planned condo-hotel building. Or $200,000 at the exchange rate at the time.

In 2015, when I negotiated a special discount for members of my *Real Estate Trend Alert* group, the price was much less. My group could have snapped up one of these condos at members-only pricing of 290,500 *reais* (less than $76,000 at the exchange rate at the time).

That was an exceptional deal. I expect this condo to rise in value when Brazil is back in fashion with investors. And, it comes with the potential for a strong rental yield in the meantime.

There's a large potential rental base for these condos; a buyer could gross up to 12% per year. It has appeal to many different types of renters. It could attract vacationers who want to spend time in Fortaleza or the middle- and upper-class workers who don't want to live or spend their weekends in a place as unappealing and busy as Pecem.

These condos, at 450 square feet, are small by North American standards. But they're perfect for a vacationer, visiting executives, or workers from Pecem. I'd figure on renting one of these for 3,000 *reais* (more than $940 at the exchange rates at time of writing) per month.

Brazil's politics will continue to ebb and flow. Commodity booms and busts will come and go. As long as your rent checks keep coming, you shouldn't care. Then when fashions circle back, commodity prices are high again, and Brazil is once more an investor's darling, your little condo could be worth $200,000. That's more than double a return on your investment. And you will have banked all those rent checks along the way.

Icarai de Amontada—Brazilian for "Cheap, Beautiful Beachfront"

Cumbuco is not the only stretch of beach I've found in Northeast Brazil that's caught my attention. A little farther away—about two-and-a-half hours from Fortaleza and two hours from Pecem—is a more frontier opportunity that could be set for a big rise in value. Right now, it's off the radar of most investors—both domestic and international real estate investors. But when I visited, I found that word was starting to get out about Icarai de Amontada, and that local businesses were already feeling the benefit.

Natchi and her husband own the biggest *pousada* (guesthouse) in town. Both are local and business is booming. Wind energy is a big deal in this part of Brazil. When I was there, mid-week during off season, the place was booked out, thanks to 45 wind-energy workers. The location of the *pousada* and the town of Icarai is convenient for them. Icarai (pronounced ick-ar-eye) is the closest town to the nearby wind farms.

But sheltered in lush vegetation and right on the empty beach, this certainly doesn't feel like a frontier energy town. It's a tropical paradise. The land here is among the best raw beachfront I've seen in a long time.

Warm breezes clear broken clouds and open up the big blue sky. The sea is a warm blue turning turquoise as gentle waves roll past. A picture-perfect vista and setting. The beach stretches almost as far as the eye can see in either direction.

Sandy points frame the horizon in both directions. In the distance, giant dunes dominate the landscape—but here in Icarai it's like a little oasis. Wild palm trees sway gently. Colorful flowers climb up walls and sprout from hedgerows. Of course, I visit lots of picturesque places. Often the most picturesque come with a high price point. But unusually, the land prices here are incredibly low. I knew when I visited that I was on to something big.

This is a location that could take off in a serious way. Because of the limited supply of available beachfront property in Icarai, a small amount of outside interest could quickly push prices up.

Natchi and her husband are sitting on pure gold. Natchi knows this beachfront has value. Her husband negotiated to buy beachfront all along here from local fishermen. The fishermen who sold saw little value in the land. Natchi's husband saw a bit more. He's diversified into leasing vehicles to the local wind farms, and is the closest thing to a real estate agent in town. So far, this is a largely untapped location. But if and when it takes off, I expect values will rise.

How to Buy the World's Best-Value Beachfront

The last time I was here, beachfront in Icarai listed for 200 *reais* per meter. At current exchange rates, that's 200,000 *reais* ($64,288) for a quarter-acre of some of the world's most spectacular true beachfront.

Those wealthy people from Fortaleza—the ones who set the trends—haven't caught on to this little place. Brazilians, like those fishermen who sold to Natchi and her husband, don't realize what makes this such a special place. Instead, demand is coming from overseas.

"Foreigners have to come into our own backyard so we can discover the true value of things," a friend explained. Ten years ago there was nothing but a local fish restaurant in Icarai. When I was there, just one beachfront mansion was under construction—the rest of the beachfront is dotted with *pousadas* and restaurants. Their owners came from France, Italy, and Switzerland.

Europeans came to Icarai because they fell for the stunning curve of beach and a charming little fishing village. They lend a classy atmosphere to the town. I believe it's only a matter a time (and not much time) before the wealthy from Fortaleza will catch on to the appeal of this place, thanks to the Europeans popularizing it.

You pretty much walk straight off the beach into the clean and tidy town square. Typical of beach towns along this coast, it has cobblestone streets and a pleasant but small, open plaza. Little streets radiate from the main plaza. The homes of traditional fishermen and a few expats make the most of the tropical gardens, with their brightly colored flowers.

This beach town is bordered on one side by wind farms and a wide river entering the ocean. Past the town on the other side, you have protected lands and wind farms. Development can't sprawl along the coast.

A Slow Discovery by European Expats

The French were the first to come to Icarai. They came and opened little cafés and restaurants. Then one Frenchman bought land and sold lots to friends back home. More French came—bringing their love of the finer things in life. And with a stronger euro against a weak *real*, there's an even greater appeal to Europeans to come.

I believe this beach town could explode in popularity—just as I have seen happen to Cumbuco and other beach towns along this coast.

When I first visited Cumbuco, it was quiet like Icarai—before Europeans discovered it. Norwegians came to retire to Cumbuco and

Scandinavian kite surfers came on vacation. Now 2,000 Koreans live there. As far as I know, there wasn't a single Korean resident when I first visited. (They work on major construction projects in Pecem.)

You can't buy beachfront in Cumbuco, as it's pretty much built out. Beachfront land outside Cumbuco could set you back over $1 million per acre.

But when I was last in the middle of picture-perfect Icarai de Amontada, you could buy a small lot, a block or two back from the beach, for as little as 37,500 *reais* ($17,000 at the exchange rates of the time).

A friend of a friend bought the lot next door. That's how I ended up here.

This part of Northeast Brazil is not undiscovered. Close to Icarai is Jericoacoara. "Jeri," as it's known locally, is another beach town with high real estate prices—Brazilians love to spend time there, but there's not much inventory in town. I've heard the few people from Fortaleza who know Icarai describe it as "the new Jeri."

Constructed Homes in Icarai

There's not much in the way of bigger construction projects in Icarai—certainly not much that I would recommend to buy.

The only planned community in Icarai I saw when I last visited consisted of four homes around a small communal pool area. With the cleaner's help, I got through the gate and had a look around one of these homes. Downstairs was an open-plan kitchen/living area and a large bedroom. Upstairs was another large bedroom under a pitched roof. The homes looked like they are used as rentals for kite surfers. But the homes were also listed for sale—as was the piece of adjoining land. The homes were listing for 300,000 *reais* ($136,000 at the exchange rates) each.

The homes aren't particularly special. They're the type of little home that would be fine for a rental but not particularly distinctive in any way. Still, there's a reason why I was interested in them. It's not because the homes are distinctive enough to cause a rise in value. If values of these homes were to rise, it's because of the appreciation of the land, rather than a rise in the value of the house on the land. In a place like this, land will appreciate at a faster rate.

The geography of Icarai is such that, once it develops, land will become extremely scarce. Beach towns like Cumbuco can spread along the coast—300 condos have been built in the past couple of years in the first phase of one condo community in Cumbuco.

That's just *one* phase, of *one* community, in *one* resort. That can't happen in Icarai because of the shortage of developable land. Even a small number of buyers from Fortaleza or foreigners buying land will make prices pop. If, say, just 60 people were to buy land to build a little home in this beach town, you'd be looking at a very high-demand, limited-inventory situation…which would make prices skyrocket from their low base.

My recommendation: Buy land in Icarai.

The Risks

There is a catch to that recommendation and it's an important one. Very little of the land in Icarai…none that I checked out…is titled. Locals just never bothered getting title, even when they could. Land transfers are made via a notary document of transfer of possession. This can be converted to a title. The process is relatively inexpensive but can take six months.

That introduces a risk and a complication into buying. If you do decide to check out Icarai and end up making an offer on land, I recommend that you write a contract subject to "titling" of the land. Write into your contract that your lawyer takes charge of the titling process. That way the seller can't renege on the deal by failing in the titling process. In a place like this, where I expect values could rise fast, you don't want to give the seller the chance to wriggle out of the deal and sell to a higher bidder.

My Recommendations for What to Buy in Icarai

When I made my initial recommendations for Icarai in July 2014, I advised three different options for buying. To be clear, the options to buy are limited—and more so since readers who followed my recommendations have snapped up some of what's on offer.

But still, Icarai remains a good buy. If you're considering checking it out for yourself, there are three ways to buy, if you find the right piece of property and a good deal.

They are:

1. Raw beachfront. There's limited land available for sale in this beach town. Only a small percentage of this is beachfront—in fact, when I made my initial recommendation in July 2014, only three beachfront lots were available for sale. The chance to buy beachfront doesn't come up often. But when it does, it can be a good deal. It's attractive to the Brazilian buyers I expect will come. Rich people from Fortaleza will only want to build their beach mansion right on the beach; so owning the piece of beachfront land they'll want to build on will put you ahead of the game.

As an example of the kind of lots that come up for sale, I put boots on the ground on two lots. Both were 25 meters wide and 52 meters deep and were priced at 260,000 *reais* ($118,000 at the exchange rate at the time) each. If you were to buy them and merge them together, you would have had a valuable beachfront land bank right on the edge of town.

It's the type of land that would be like gold for a developer who wanted to build a condo project or a hotel.

The pricing was about average when I visited. I found that 200 *reais* per meter is the price for beachfront land that everyone seems to quote—regardless of the land's proportions. Of course, the more beachfront, the better.

2. Lots in a subdivision. I saw one subdivision of 16 lots. They had sold out for 25,000 *reais* ($11,500 at the exchange rate at the time). The lots were 250 square meters; that's 100 *reais* per meter. I wasn't disappointed to miss this one. There were no covenants or restrictions. There's nothing to stop a metal shop opening in the lot next to yours.

But still, the right lot in a subdivision could be a great buy. As I've said, land is limited in town.

There are even fewer land parcels big enough to accommodate a planned community, so land suitable for a small community would also be a great buy. With a buy of just 4 acres, you'd have room for roads and 24 little lots.

3. Lots in town. Icarai is a pretty, safe, clean, and charming beach town. Owning a lot in town, with a view to build on it, could be a good buy. When I visited, you could buy lots on a quiet side street just a few blocks from the main town square and beach. Next door to you would be local fishermen, European-owned *pousadas*, and second homes. One deal I found was a 500-square-meter lot for 37,000 *reais* ($17,000 at the time). Plenty of space to build a comfortable home.

If You're Offered a Dead Chicken in Brazil, Take It

"You need to check out this 'dead chicken,' Ronan," my real estate contact in Brazil told me as we pulled up to a luxury condo.

I wondered whether I had heard him right. I had just stepped off a plane from Lisbon and the jet lag was catching up with me. I was baffled for a moment.

"What did you say?"

He looked at me in exasperation. "A 'dead chicken.'" When I still looked baffled, he explained, "A 'dead chicken' is an easy meal. You don't have to go chasing after it and kill it."

Translation: This was an easy deal—or what we might call "low-hanging fruit." He explained that it was a term used locally to describe no-brainer real estate deals that come up from time to time. The kinds of deals that happen when folks have to sell fast because of a special situation. When folks are willing to sell way below market value to sell quickly.

"Dead chickens" are something I pay close attention to in Brazil. They can be a killer deal when you find one. And, because of Brazil's current economic crisis, there's some strong opportunity to buy at dead-chicken pricing, even in Brazil's up-and-coming Northeast.

You may have seen headlines out of Brazil that talk about the country's recession. It's the worst in two decades. But the economic crisis hasn't hit the country evenly. In the south, which is the country's most prosperous region, the effects of the recession are being felt hard.

In the Northeast, which I've been keeping a close eye on for close to a decade, the story is different. It's been growing at breakneck speed for the past 20 years. And the case for Northeast Brazil hasn't changed. It's still a region on the up...

one where a savvy investor could do well buying undervalued real estate...and benefit as real estate values grow.

But as I write this, the current crisis is creating opportunity—especially for dead-chicken deals. Even though Northeast Brazil isn't feeling the effects of the crisis like the south, people aren't buying. That's a typical reaction in times of crisis. People get nervous about the future. And when they're nervous, they don't spend. Right now, the market has stalled.

That means that there are bargains to be found from sellers who, for personal reasons, need to sell quickly.

Right now, people in Northeast Brazil who want to sell fast will sell for 25% below market value. Selling at market value today takes six to eight months—no good for a seller who needs a quick sale. So they're forced to drop their prices even lower. That creates an opportunity to buy distressed real estate at an even deeper discount.

One recent dead-chicken deal that came up was in the beach city of Fortaleza—Brazil's most popular domestic tourism destination. In 2014, it got more than four million tourists.

An owner was selling a spacious and luxurious condo right on the boardwalk. It is more than 1,900 square feet... so large it takes up its own floor. It has stunning views to the ocean. Before the crisis, you could easily have expected to pay 3 million *reais* ($1.5 million) for a condo like this. But the owner listed it for 1.9 million *reais*. He needed to sell fast. He got fast cash but only 950,000 *reais*. That's not much more than $250,000 for a primo condo in a world-class city in the middle of a medium-term upswing.

The best dead-chicken deals go quickly. If you don't hear about them in time, chances are you'll miss out. That's why I've cultivated a little black book of contacts in Brazil and elsewhere—so I'm the first to hear of the best dead-chicken deals as they happen.

CHAPTER 5:

Location #3: Where You Could Potentially Double Your Money in 5 Years—Ireland

I could already see the lush green fields as the plane started its descent into Dublin airport. To the left of the fields, the twinkling lights of boats in Dublin Bay blinked like a welcoming beacon.

Though I get to see some of the most stunning destinations in the world on my scouting trips—I spend about half the year on the road—I breathe a sigh of contentment when I arrive back in Ireland.

I may be a little biased. Ireland, after all, is the country where I grew up. But to me, it is one of the best places in the world and will always be where I call home.

Even in its cities, strangers will stop to chat to you in grocery stores, in pubs, or as you wait in line at the bank. They don't want anything from you: They're just a chatty, friendly, largely helpful people.

And this is a place that's home to some of Europe's best attractions. Crumbling ruins of castles dot the landscape around the country. In the summertime, the hedgerows and flowering trees that line the secondary roads burst into color. When you want the best of city life, you can head to the capital, Dublin, or to Cork, Galway, or Limerick. If you're looking to escape the city, you can be in the wilds of Connemara in the west or along the Atlantic coast in the southwest in easy time. Any option won't take you long. Because Ireland is so small, the farthest point away from you will rarely be more than six hours' drive.

As I stepped off the plane, I was looking forward to the *craic* (fun) and easygoing pace Ireland is famous for, but also because of the real estate opportunities that were on my radar.

Ireland's Real Estate Crisis Opportunity

The opportunity in Europe to buy low and double your money has rarely been greater than in the past decade. Ireland has offered some of the best opportunities of all.

Ireland is a real estate market I have a lot of experience in. It's the country that I come from, where I was educated, and where I started my investment journey. I've had the benefit, if you can call it that, of a front row seat to its boom—and its bust. Now the market is rallying again and real estate prices are starting to rise.

Ireland's meteoric economic rise was the stuff of headlines worldwide. Newspapers the world over were talking about the country's "Celtic Tiger"—a period of unprecedented economic growth that started in the 1990s.

Thanks to inward investment, some business-friendly government policy, and growing income levels, the country took off. Spiraling real estate prices weren't far behind.

In the early and mid-2000s, Europe's real estate markets embarked on a massive tear. Ireland's was one of its fastest growing real estate markets. In just one decade, between 1997 and 2007, prices for new houses increased by more than 200%. (No, that's not a misplaced zero—that 200% figure is correct.) Already built homes sold for even more. The increase was a whopping 280%!

But, just as in the U.S., many of those real estate sales were funded by cheap credit. And, as anyone with even a passing interest in the U.S. real estate market of the 2000s will know, cheap credit isn't always a good thing. When allowed to grow out of control, you have the makings of a bubble. A bubble that will inevitably burst.

Values were getting out of control in Ireland. Buying was fueled by media, with people influenced by glossy spreads in magazines and pages-long real estate sections in national newspapers. Everyone wanted a piece of the pie—and they borrowed more and more to do it. People who at one time were happy to own their own house free and clear re-financed, often to buy a vacation home or make a speculative investment in Europe's sunnier locales.

It became a gold rush. A mad frenzy not to miss. A lot of people thought that values would never stop rising—until everything stopped.

The market imploded and real estate owners found themselves deep under water.

It takes time after a crisis like this for the real bargain buys to emerge. That's because of human nature. People don't immediately start selling up when they realize that trouble has hit. A lot of them will dig their heels in and wait for things to get better.

The psychology of a distressed real estate market is a lot like a grieving process. There are various stages of denial and anger until acceptance is reached—acceptance that your real estate is only worth what someone is willing to pay for it. People with hefty mortgages take time to come to the realization that they've made a bad investment. So for a few years after Ireland's crisis began, the real estate market largely stalled. People and property developers in debt were still pricing their property too highly, hoping that someone would bite.

When the Market Started Moving Again

The crash started in Ireland in 2008. But it took another four years for prices to reach their lowest point.

That's partly because of a difference in how U.S. bankruptcy and European bankruptcy works. Europe doesn't have a quick, clean bankruptcy process. Foreclosures are difficult legally—especially difficult in Ireland. Banks were slow to foreclose even when they legally could, because there's a lot of public resistance. The banks were also slow to acknowledge that the property they held on their books was worth a lot less than the values they had logged on their balance sheets.

It took a long time for the distress to be reflected in Ireland's property prices.

When real estate transactions just stop, something needs to happen to bring activities back to the market—a liquidity-triggering event. In the case of Ireland, that was the arrival of distressed real estate auctions in 2011.

This was quite the price-discovery process. Sellers finally realized how little buyers were willing to pay. It brought liquidity to the market. Ireland was the first of Europe's real estate markets to slide into crisis. Ireland was then the first market to show signs of liquidity and recovery. The real estate market in Ireland stayed "no-bid" until fire sale auctions came to the market in April 2011.

I recognized it as the time for international real estate buyers to act. I could see recovery was coming, but prices were still falling. It created a window of opportunity that was too good to resist. The case for buying was strongest in Dublin City, the country's capital, which was recovering the fastest from the crisis.

I recommended condos close to Dublin's financial services center and city center. The case was compelling. Ireland was in crisis, but these locations were still attracting companies like Google, LinkedIn, and Airbnb. Some sectors were losing jobs, while this mobile multinational sector continued to show strong growth.

Employment in Dublin's financial services center remained robust. Dublin was still a vibrant university city and the country's capital. Values on the condos I recommended at €140,000 in 2011 have risen by 60% or more. Rents have increased from levels that already commanded double-digit yields. A buyer who bought one of those condos in 2011 could easily double his money by now—from a mix of capital appreciation and rental income.

The moment has passed in Dublin. It's currently seeing another mini-bubble. Prices are rising and it's once again too rich for my blood. But there is still opportunity in other parts of Ireland.

What Happened to Ireland's Pre-Construction Deals?

Before Ireland's real estate bubble took off in earnest, it was possible and not unusual for buyers to buy pre-construction—that is, to buy solely off architectural plans with a down payment, and to make payments as the home was being built.

This type of buying is still common around the world, especially in many deals I scout out in Latin America. It's seen as a win-win for a lot of developers: They get to lock down sales in the earlier phases of development and help to finance the build with those pre-construction sales, rather than taking out a bank loan.

But Ireland's developers got greedy during the boom. Instead of selling some of their properties pre-construction—and using the money to offset building costs—they decided to become speculators. Instead of releasing pre-construction deals to market, they held the properties back. It worked in their favor for a little while. They were speculating that their finished project would have accumulated in value during the build process. For some time, they were right. Until the market crashed.

That's how so many big developers got into major difficulties. They, too, were taking advantage of cheap credit to finance their builds. So when the market went no-bid, they were left with a mountain of debt...and with finished projects they couldn't hope to sell for the margins they expected. Many of them went under, and dozens of so-called "ghost estates" (finished or partially-finished housing projects) were left to fall into disrepair.

The Housing Crisis in Dublin Right Now

The crisis that faces Dublin now is something new. Far from having a glut of housing to buy or rent, there now aren't enough homes for people to buy or rent. Rents have risen dramatically. More people are renting today than ever before, because many of them can't afford to buy. The rental rates are rising again. In fact, rental rates in key markets like central Dublin today are higher than they were at the peak of the market in 2006.

A friend owns a little cottage of less than 700 square feet in central Dublin. He advertised it on a rental website. His ad lasted seven hours before he had to take it down. The ad had more than 900 views, my friend had over 30 calls, and 15 confirmed viewings for his open house on the following Sunday.

Most interestingly, he received multiple offers of additional cash if he would take the house off the market before the open house.

The rental shortage has worsened since then. There's a housing crisis. There aren't enough homes available in the locations where people want to buy or rent. This supply shortage isn't easy to fix.

At the heart of the problem are supply shortages and supply constraints. The supply constraints are permitting and protection regulations. Dublin's desirable areas are typically wide, tree-lined streets dotted with protected historic housing that you can't knock down. And there are limited opportunities for infill. Secondly, where you have green-field sites, development can be challenging. The permitting process is long, drawn out, and expensive.

And high-rise building isn't common in Ireland. Much of the zoning doesn't allow for it.

Additionally, there's a lot of land around Dublin that has permits. But the land is tied up in bankruptcy processes post-crisis. Or the permitting includes a mix of homes and condos. The market is looking for homes. According to the permitting, you can't build the homes if you don't build the condos.

Because of all that, it's not a market I want to play. Instead, I'm looking at the hidden—even hated—places where the underlying fundamentals are still strong.

Play the "Hated Sector" to See Your Investment Double

I still see an opportunity for profit in Ireland. But it's off the radar of the mega-groups buying up in Dublin. The big idea surrounds apartment rentals in secondary cities and big towns. It's a hated sector—a sector that's still licking its wounds. Investors lost their shirts as values tanked by 80% or even more. Banks got burnt. The quality of tenants went down as supply increased. Rents fell and became more difficult to collect. A whole generation of landlords, beaten down, gave up or retreated to managing what they had. No one wants to be in this business now.

The effect is hardest on some buyers who only became landlords at the height of the frenzy. They bought second homes without ever thinking of the work involved—or the stress they would be under with two mortgages they couldn't afford. They're over-extended, struggling under debt, and keen to get out of the landlord game.

These days, no one wants to be in this business—at least not in the secondary cities: places like Cork and Limerick in the south and Galway in the west. So that creates a small buying moment. People who want—or need—to get out from under debt are selling for a fraction of what they bought. But the economy in those secondary cities and big towns is improving quickly. The rental markets are back, particularly near major hospitals, universities, and colleges.

Buy really cheap, play this market, and you could do well. That could come from buying from a distressed seller, or picking up something really cheaply at a fire-sale auction. To be clear, fire-sale auctions aren't nearly as common now as they were in 2011 through 2013, and the big bargains are harder to find. But they do still come up from time to time.

At a previous fire-sale auction, a little block of eight apartments and duplexes in the city of Limerick, in the mid-west, came under the hammer with a reserve of €380,000. The winning buyer bid €475,000. Even at that higher price point, the buyer got himself a great deal. Replacement cost for a building like this would be in the region of €1 million. That deal was three years ago, and those condos are already well on track to doubling in value. By the time the five-year mark has passed, you'd have doubled your money on capital appreciation alone. But there's another sweetener: rental income.

The units are close to the University of Limerick, Limerick Institute of Technology, and about 10 minutes from Limerick regional hospital. There is always demand for rentals from the educated professionals working or studying in the hospital or education institutes. They were sold as rental-ready. They would realistically rent for €62,000 per year. If you'd bought them and invested another €100,000 to upgrade them, you could ask for a higher rental rate: They could throw off €80,000 a year.

On rental income alone, if you had acted on that opportunity without investing a cent in upgrades, you could have seen substantial gains quickly. At full occupancy of those eight units, you could have targeted a gross rental yield of €62,000 per year. Over five years, that's a potential gross yield of €310,000. If you'd upgraded them, to target a gross yield of €80,000 a year, you'd gross €400,000 in five years. That's almost the entire cost of your initial purchase price back—and that's presuming rental rates won't increase. (Current trends seem to indicate that they most definitely will.) Coupled with the strong capital appreciation you would have seen in just the first three years alone, this has proven itself a standout opportunity.

Demographics and employment trends will keep driving demand for a building like this. Development is slowly coming back to Ireland. But outside Dublin, it's at nowhere near the rate that the country saw during the economic boom. New projects are slow to come online, so at the moment, there isn't much competition from new rentals. Not until developers can build and sell them at a commercially viable price.

Playing this crisis angle doesn't require a big investment. You don't need a half-million euro or more to get in.

In the city center of Cork, I found a more recent opportunity to take advantage of this play. It's a great location—one of Ireland's prettiest cities in the south of the country. It's got a serious rental shortage. And if you know how to play this shortage, you could still do well in Ireland.

In September 2015, I told members of *Real Estate Trend Alert* about six homes that were listed for sale in Cork City center. These were foreclosure sales—the agent was pushing for a batch sale. At the time, it would have cost you €350,000 ($394,800) for the six properties: Four listed for €65,000 ($73,300), one for €75,000 ($84,600), and one for €70,000 ($78,950).

I suggested an additional €20,000 ($22,560) per property for renovations and furniture. Your total investment would have been €470,000 ($530,200). I said in September 2015 that I expected the value to climb to €1.1 million in seven years. They're well on track to achieving that figure.

At a current value of €150,000 per home, as of January 2017 (so a total of $900,000 for all six homes), that's a potential capital appreciation of €550,000 in less than two years—they're well on track to doubling in value within five years.

Add to that the rental yield you'd have banked (you could rent one of these homes long-term for €850 per month) and you're looking at an additional €61,000 ($68,650) per year in gross rental income.

Opportunity like this still comes up if you know the right way to buy. If you buy distressed (or something unloved—see sidebar below), you could still pick up a cottage for €60,000. Spend €20,000 on refurbishment and furnishing and you could rent it out for €800 a month. That's a gross yield of 12% a year. And values in Cork are on the rise. From Q1 2015 to Q1 2016, property values in Cork City increased by 14.9%. From Q1 2016 to Q4 2016, it increased again by 12.1%.

Buying well in Ireland isn't the easy pickings it once was. To do well here now, you have to do your homework—pick up something unloved and overlooked. But it's still possible. In Chapter 12, I'll tell you about one of the most recent ways I've found to play this market—by buying something unloved and low-priced at auction and renting it out.

Buy a Piece of Romantic Ireland

I'm in the business of finding real estate deals with a strong capital appreciation or a rental income angle. But occasionally, a deal catches my eye that, while undervalued, isn't a particularly incredible deal from an investor's perspective. These are deals that are great buys for a person looking for a piece of real estate they can enjoy in person.

Some of Ireland's historic properties and vacation homes both fall into this category. They're not for every investor. But if you're looking for a passion project—a place to renovate, like one of its neglected historical properties—or just a comfortable home in a stunning location to spend time in, they could be for you.

Historic Homes

In the years following the economic crisis, bargain historical properties were easy to find. Many had fallen into disrepair. They were owned by people who couldn't afford to pay for the upkeep necessary to keep a property like this in good shape.

During the crisis, I found an opportunity to buy a 10,000-square-foot historic house on 68 acres of land for €750,000 ($960,000 at exchange rates at the time). It was a no-brainer deal: The land was worth more than the asking price. You could have sold most of the land off at a profit—and owned the historic home and a substantial portion of land, for nothing.

But though the opportunities aren't so common now, they do still come up—often at auctions. Last year, a 19th-century house, in Italian neo-classical style, came to auction. The house itself is massive, spreading out over almost 8,900 square feet. It's set in 9.6 acres of land, in a small village with good road and rail connections to Dublin, around 40 miles away.

Back in 2008, this house and land were on sale for €4.5 million. By 2010, the price was down to €1.25 million. But in April last year, the house—which had been allowed to fall into disrepair, with parts of the roof missing and the windows boarded up—finally sold at auction for just $440,000—less than 10% of its original asking price.

Vacation Homes and Rural Cottages

When things were good, a different sort of property ownership took off in Ireland: the ownership of a second home as a vacation property. It wasn't unheard of before the Celtic Tiger for a rare few to own a vacation home. But when cheap credit was introduced and the middle class started to grow, so too did the sale of vacation homes and traditional farm cottages.

But matters have largely returned to what they were before. The locals don't see the value in older, more traditional housing. They opt to build a new house rather than renovate a traditional farmhouse or cottage. And there is almost no demand from Irish people to buy a vacation home. They are happy to rent when they want to use one.

Values plummeted on both newer vacation properties and on traditional farmhouses and cottages in the recession. Many owners who had borrowed heavily to buy a place needed to sell—and fast. Values hit rock bottom in Ireland's most scenic locales along the coastlines and in Ireland's lake country.

In 2014, homes of this type were going for silly-cheap prices. There was just no market for them. No one was interested in buying a traditional farmhouse or cottage—even one that sat on a few acres with ocean views.

In the untamed wild beauty of West Cork I found a particularly great deal: a typical Irish farm cottage listed for €85,000 ($108,500 at exchange rates at the time). I recommended offering €70,000 ($89,300 at the time). The farm cottage is a short stroll from the ocean and has great views to the ocean and headland beyond from the upper floor. The ground floor had been updated by the seller but the second story was a blank canvas. With an extra spend of $25,000 and a little time and imagination, you could create a charming, picture-perfect little Irish farm cottage on its own ocean-view plot.

You might see some rental income from a place like this, but due to its location, I wouldn't recommend relying on that income. Instead, this is the kind of property that you can enjoy for yourself and maybe rent out when you're not using it.

Vacation homes and traditional rural cottages with views still come to market from time to time now. And they still haven't returned to the high prices of the economic boom. With a bit of searching, there are still bargains to be found.

CHAPTER 6:

Location #4: Where You Could Potentially Double Your Money in 5 Years—Spain

Ireland was not the only country in Europe hit hard by the global recession—or the only European country where I've seen opportunity to double your investment. In fact, five countries were so badly affected that they earned the colorful (and often seen as derogatory) acronym PIIGS. That stands for Portugal, Italy, Ireland, Greece, and Spain.

As I told you earlier in this book (and as I'll expand on in Chapter 11), the wake of a crisis is often the best time to find seriously undervalued real estate. I kept a close eye on all those countries to see how the crisis opportunity would play out. Ireland, as you've just read, eventually presented plentiful opportunity for real estate investors.

Of the others, Italy offered a sparse handful of opportunities, but not so many that I could get behind it as a real estate investment play. Greece is still a basket case—there's no opportunity so far. Portugal, in the past two years, is starting to yield major opportunities in certain areas.

But of them all, none has been so compelling or as profitable for savvy real estate investors as Spain.

I like Spain. I've spent a lot of time there in recent years. For three years in a row, I've marked St. Patrick's Day on her Costa del Sol. Three days after St. Patrick's Day this year, I headed to Picasso's home city of Málaga to watch the Palm Sunday parade. They don't mess around in Spain when it comes to religious celebrations. They favor pomp and ceremony, much as you see in Latin America. Men in red hoods and white robes followed an ornate statue of Jesus held high. The tradition of wearing those hoods dates back to medieval times. It's definitely a spectacle that sticks with you.

Day-to-day life in Spain is enjoyable. The food is good…the beers cold and cheap…and the sunshine, at least in the Costa del Sol, plentiful.

But the pleasures of Spain were not enough to keep her economy in good shape. The last eight years have seen the country take a fiscal pummeling.

Spain, like Ireland, was hit hard when the recession rolled through. Before the crisis hit in 2008, the economy was largely fueled by development. You could see it when you visited: Cranes dotted the skyline and countless new developments were underway at any given time.

But then, as in Ireland, the bottom fell out of the market. Banks started to fail. Unemployment climbed. The real estate market went no-bid. I knew in 2008 that there would be opportunity; the question was when. I watched the market closely, waiting for the trigger event that would mean opportunity for real estate investors.

I waited five years for real estate prices to reflect Spain's crisis.

The fallout of the recession was dramatic. The banks and the government were broke. They'd overextended themselves, borrowing and lending too much. They were buried under a mountain of debt. By 2013, unemployment rates were topping a record 26%. Young people were even more badly affected: Youth unemployment rates hit north of 50%. Many had no option but to leave for other countries; there were simply no jobs for them.

The biggest problem with the real estate market was a question of numbers. There were too many homes and properties to sell and not enough people to buy them. At one point, estimates put Spain's excess supply of homes between 1 and 2 million. That's a lot of property—with no buyers to take them.

The young people who might once have owned an entry-level home either couldn't afford one or were forced to move away. Immigration slowed down, too. That makes sense when you think about it: If there weren't jobs for the young, there certainly weren't any for immigrants.

And what about the foreign buyers who tended to own a vacation property in Spain's vacation destinations? Many of them were facing their own economic crises back home. They were reluctant to spend money on a purchase overseas. They were waiting to see how problems facing their own economies would play out and to see how Spain's real estate market would go. The smarter buyers were waiting to see how far prices would fall before buying in Spain. That was a sensible move. Immediately following the crash, prices stagnated. It made no sense to buy in 2008 and 2009, while prices had so much further to drop.

All those factors meant that, for several years, absorption of Spain's oversupply was impossible. For those with jobs, particularly the young who would typically pick up this slack, incomes were so low that, even when prices dropped 30% to 70% below peak 2008 prices, buying a home was still beyond their reach. (That's still the case for many of those young people today.)

The Trigger Moment I Was Waiting For

I held off on making any recommendations in Spain for several years after its crisis hit. The numbers didn't stack up yet.

To put it simply, the whole country was in calamity. Spain was in no way prepared for the crisis. It blindsided the country. Nobody was quite sure how to deal with the mess left behind. So for a while, they did nothing. They held onto the hope that things would improve by themselves. The banks and developers, rather than offloading the real estate on their books cheaply, instead tried to ride out the storm. They waited for buyers to come back and to pay the over-inflated prices they'd been able to charge just before the crisis. There were no buyers—especially none with the money to spend on overpriced condos and houses. So, the market stagnated.

The market was waiting for one moment—one trigger event—to restart. It was 2012 before it got one.

In 2012, the Spanish government approved the setting up of a so-called "bad bank," SAREB. Its creation was the event I'd been waiting for.

SAREB's aim was to stabilize the market. It took on a raft of property development loans from Spanish banks. And it was given 15 years to dispose of all those loans and the properties on its books. The quickest way to do that: fire-sale auctions.

The bank rolled out the first of these bank fire-sales in the summer of 2013. And there were some major discounts up for grabs.

Not everything offered first was a buy. In fact, in typical bureaucratic style, the approach to pricing made no sense to an outsider. It was insane. For many of the properties put up for sale, the price was decided by a banker sitting in an office hundreds of miles away. He decided the reserve price based on a spreadsheet in front of him. In many cases, the person deciding the pricing never even visited the property he was selling! That meant that some properties released were seriously overpriced for what they were...and some incredible real estate was incredibly undervalued.

From those bank fire-sales, I found some great opportunities to profit in the last three years. SAREB was successful in its goal. It has sold off much of its inventory in the four years since it was formed. These days, the opportunities to buy a fire-sale property well are fewer and fewer. Still, the odd bargain can be found—if you know where to look.

The Best Opportunities I've Found to Double Your Money in Spain

Though I've found strong opportunities in Spain, I need to be clear: The country as a whole is not a buy. There are still large swathes of Spain that I would never consider buying in. The macro story for their recovery isn't compelling; their growth trajectory is too slow and uncertain to make them worth a recommendation.

But there is one area where I've found plentiful opportunity: the region in southern Spain called the "Costa del Sol." The Costa del Sol is—and has been for decades—Spain's tourist and expat haven. As the name might suggest (it translates to "Sun Coast"), this is one of Spain's sunniest areas. It gets an average of 325 days of sunshine a year.

This is Europe's sunbelt. The trends enticing people here are growing stronger. Like that in the U.S., Europe's population is aging. Europe's baby boomers, in particular those from the north, are looking for their place in the sun. Thanks to technology, business people, freelancers, and employees are more mobile than ever before. The Costa del Sol is centered around Marbella, a place pulling people in from all over the world.

And the charms of Andalucía—which embodies the stereotypical image of Spain with its flamenco, bullfighting, and white-washed villages—is all around. Little wonder that Andalucía—particularly the Costa del Sol—is one of Spain's most popular tourist destinations. Tourism is big business for Spain; it accounts for about 11% of the country's GDP. In 2015, more than 68 million vacationers visited Spain, making it the third-most visited country in the world. And the Costa del Sol is where the tourism machine is at its finest and most developed.

But in the wake of the crisis, it was seriously affected. Development zoomed ahead in the years leading up to 2008—with more property aimed at renting to vacationers and selling to foreigners who want to own a second home in the sun.

When the market dried up, so too did sales on the Costa del Sol. The number of foreign buyers dwindled. Much of the inventory available wasn't targeted at the local market. The real estate that was suitable for locals still struggled to find buyers: Spain's high unemployment meant they couldn't afford what was on offer.

Prices plummeted along the Costa del Sol. Within SAREB's fire-sale inventory was a lot of real estate here. By 2013, you could buy close to the beach for as little as one-third of 2009 pricing…but those same properties could generate rental yields of 8% at 50% occupancy. That's because tourists were still coming to the Costa del Sol. The market for rentals was still there. But the buyers for these properties were not.

SAREB has successfully offloaded a good chunk of the Costa del Sol inventory. Deals still come up, but they're few and far between these days.

Outside of SAREB, there are still good deals to be had. Many sellers in this region just want out and to move on.

Spain's economy is in bounce-back mode. It's rallying after eight years of uncertainty and is showing signs of growth. The economy grew by 3.2% in 2015 and unemployment has dropped to around 17%. Final figures for 2016 had yet to be confirmed at the time of writing, but all indicators say that Spain's growth last year outstripped most other EU countries.

That means the window of opportunity is rapidly closing for smart real estate investors here. In the next couple of years, I expect the opportunity—outside of some rare situations or special deals—to have completely passed. And the pickings are a lot fewer than they were in 2013 to 2015. But if you can find the right property at the right undervalued pricing, you could do well here, as members of my *Real Estate Trend Alert* group have done with my recommendations.

In 2014, I recommended condos in an established community on the Costa del Sol for €150,000. They were in San Pedro del Alcántara. An underpass had just been completed there two years earlier. It was cutting down on traffic and making travel to the area easier and quicker. On top of the underpass, a vast green area was being developed, making it attractive to visitors and locals.

I said these condos were a buy at €150,000. The location was good and demand was higher, thanks to the easier access. I was right about the growing demand: Today, a couple of blocks away from that community, major U.K. developer Taylor Wimpey is selling pre-construction, two-bedroom condos with prices starting in the €400,000 range.

Also in 2014, I recommended a condo in a private community less than 10 minutes from Puerto Banús, a town on a marina frequented by the rich and glamorous. The private community was in a charming location—along a tree-lined street where couples and friends dined al fresco at the many cafés and restaurants.

The developer had gotten into trouble and the bank had to step in. They started to release the condos in the community for €129,000. At the time, I predicted they'd hit the €250,000 range within five years. I was too conservative. In less than three years' time, one of those condos listed for €259,000—more than double the initial investment.

Golf: The Next Opportunity to Profit on the Costa del Sol

The Costa del Sol has another nickname you might not have heard of: the Costa del Golf. That's thanks to the massive number of golf courses along this coast. There are more than 70 between the Costa del Sol and the city of Málaga alone.

That may be part of why I like Spain so much. Anyone who knows me will know that I'm an avid golfer. I get out on the course whenever I can. The Costa del Sol offers plenty of opportunity.

But besides my personal appreciation for the sport, there's another reason why I'm so keen on golf in the Costa del Sol: Owning a home on or near a golf course can be a good investment (if you find the right property at the right price). It can mean a strong rental kicker.

A buy that ticks those boxes—potential for capital appreciation and rental income—is what I look for when I'm scouting. And that's what I found earlier this year in one project on the Costa del Sol. In fact, it's one of the strongest opportunities I've ever found in this area.

Golf is big business on the Costa del Sol. And for anyone looking for a property to rent out to a vacationer, appealing to the golf crowd can be a good idea. For rental income, you have to know who your target market is before you buy. You have to know someone is willing to pay to rent your place.

The typical vacation season for the Costa del Sol—the vacationers who come for beach and sunshine—runs from the start of June until the end of September. But the golfing sector adds a shoulder season, a month each side, to that vacation season. If you're looking for strong occupancy on a vacation home on the Costa del Sol, the golf market is a smart market to target.

Last year, I discovered an opportunity to play both that golf and vacationer market in a luxury golf community about a 35-minute drive from the high-end tourist destination of Marbella. The golf course here is one of the best I've seen. I'd put it on a par with Augusta or Valderrama.

There's more to the resort community than the 18-hole course. On site there's a luxury hotel. Angelina Jolie and Brad Pitt (when they were a couple) were guests, as was Patrick Stewart. There are varied restaurants (including a Michelin-starred Japanese restaurant), a beach club, and spa, along with residential areas. In one of those residential areas, I found an opportunity to potentially double your investment: a luxury condo that's seriously undervalued and that could offer a strong rental yield.

This is the ultimate in luxury buys: one of the premier golfing destinations and communities in all of Spain. Golfers come from all over Europe to play at Finca Cortesin—and they're willing to pay handsomely for the chance to stay close to the course.

The condos are like nothing else I've seen in Spain; they're set in an oasis of luxury, right on the Path of Progress rolling west from Marbella along the coast toward the Rock of Gibraltar. They're away from the crowded "pack 'em in" budget vacation destinations.

The developer is another of Spain's "hard luck" stories. He overextended himself in other parts of Spain and his business went under. The company that's taken these condos over is willing to sell them at seriously undervalued pricing. Pricing that I predict will rise strongly.

I didn't find this opportunity by chance. In fact, it was only by repeatedly having boots on the ground in Spain and pounding the pavement…by looking in the places others weren't looking…that I uncovered this deal. As I've said to you, this kind of on-the-ground research is essential for a good real estate scout. It's how you uncover the deals that nobody else does.

Information didn't come easily about this opportunity. It took time and a lot of phone calls and digging deeper to get the full picture about these luxury condos. But all that time and research was worth it to find what I'd call one of the best deals I've ever found in Spain.

What I found was a luxury, standout condo priced at €230,000 that I would call a €500,000 condo—a condo that's set to rise to reach its true value and where a buyer could make a strong rental income from the golfer and vacationer markets. When these condos reach their true value, a buyer will have more than doubled his/her investment. And that's before you even count a penny in rental income.

There's no competition among the other owners yet. You could easily charge €100 to €200 a night, depending on the season, for this condo. With the strong vacationer and golf market in the area, that's just the cherry on top of an incredible deal.

What's Next for Spain

Spain, like Ireland, has recovered well in recent years from its recession—and prices are rebounding. I expect the window of opportunity will close here soon, maybe in the next year. But there are "last gasp" opportunities to be found here at killer pricing. I'm keeping my eye closely on Spain. I'm still putting in the ground work and paying close attention to the situation on the ground. I'm not expecting a return any time soon to the proliferation of deals we saw at the start of the release of bank fire-sales any time soon. But that doesn't mean the opportunity is over. I predict we'll see a handful of killer deals in the next year—including opportunities where you could still stand to double your money in five years.

Right now, my attention is focused on the thousands-year-old city of Málaga. Though the crisis is nearly over for the rest of the Costa del Sol, the opportunity is not over in Málaga. I've been working on a deal here for the past year. It's slow going—I'm still digging through the red tape and bureaucracy that's holding up a killer deal. I'm expecting to put the finishing touches on that deal in the coming months.

Opportunity Coming Down the Track in Málaga

The Costa del Sol, beautiful as it is, has struggled with a mixed reputation for many years. For a long time, it was known as a place where visitors from northern climes came for cheap beer and sunshine (an unfair reputation that didn't reflect most of the Costa del Sol's reality). And the city of Málaga, just up the eastern coast from better-known Marbella, had an even worse reputation. It was the place even those "cheap beer and sunshine" visitors wanted to avoid—a dirty, grimy, and crime-ridden port city.

Around 13 million passengers per year landed in Málaga airport to head west along the coast to the beaches, golf courses, and English pubs. They didn't even think about visiting Málaga. It seemed as though this ancient city had been lost: 2,800 years of human settlement decaying.

But Málaga wasn't done. Far from it. An astonishing gentrification began, a reinvention of the old and the creation of a shiny, sleek new city. Today Málaga is on the must-visit lists of plenty of travel guides. And it's a city where you can make a killing by renting to tourists who come for a city break.

In 2015, Málaga city greeted 6 million visitors. I expect this city will become one of Europe's great weekend destinations. Málaga's appeal is broadening. I'm told (by people who pay attention to these things) that there's great shopping, and that this is a great city to party. And, unlike Prague or Paris, it has year-round warm sunshine.

There's more going on than the shopping or the weather. Málaga's grimy port area has been completely transformed into a clean, modern, waterfront district. It's true, modern, waterfront living. This is where folks come to run, read, paint, or work from a sleek new café. And where the cruise ships dock.

Málaga now feels creative, vibrant, and innovative. And it's completely bucking Spain's trend of emigration, unemployment, and deterioration. The young and funky aren't just visitors and artists. The young and ambitious are being attracted here from across the country to work in the many technology companies—from start-ups to global giants like Huawei—that have set up in a commercial district outside town.

Málaga has the startup vibrancy I saw in Berlin in 2005. There's a movement of tech companies and bureaucrats with the stated agenda of making Málaga "the Silicon Valley of Europe." That might be a tad ambitious—Spain's labor laws and bureaucracy will dispatch successful start-ups onward to Malta, Ireland, or Berlin. But it will still make a difference to this city on the Mediterranean. Málaga has set out its stall as a city for art and culture. Galleries and artists have set up in the warren of pedestrian streets that weave their way through the old town.

The city is most famous as the birthplace of renowned painter and sculptor Pablo Picasso. While he only spent the first 10 years of his life here, they named the airport after him. And you'll find a museum dedicated to his life and work. Old, abandoned historic buildings are now galleries, shops, cafés, and restaurants.

The city has made space available cheap or free for new ventures. While the main drag around Calle Larios is now premium retail real estate, this trend continues in other locales a few blocks away—like the Soho area. The foodies are here. Dotted around Málaga are a number of top-class cooking schools. This brings aspiring and established chefs to the area. The blank canvas, and cheap rents in Málaga, have given them the chance to set up shop. A place that was a cultural and culinary wilderness has quickly become one of Europe's rich bohemian cities.

Word is out. And Málaga is easily accessible, too. You can get here from right across northern Europe in two-and-a-half hours—budget airline Ryanair is one of the most frequent carriers to land here. You can fly in for less than the price of a steak dinner back home. And when visitors get here, they find a quality food and cultural experience at a fraction of the cost of northern Europe.

Málaga is changing into a world-class destination. That's important to real estate investors. This could be a place to do very well, indeed. A place where you could potentially double your investment.

The banks are still holding on to some fire-sale price opportunities—condos that are deeply discounted on peak prices (which were never that high in Málaga compared to Spain's other major cities). So soon you'll be able to buy something at silly-low pricing in a location that's on the up. The play is to buy a condo in the old town, and make it available for short-term rental.

Buy at the coming fire-sale moment and you could enjoy the post-fire-sale bounce-back in values. Then enjoy further capital appreciation as Málaga's growth trajectory continues. And bank some strong short-term rental income along the way.

I'm keeping a close eye on Málaga—and if you're interested in potentially doubling your money in real estate, you should be, too.

CHAPTER 7:

Location #5: Where You Could Potentially Double Your Money in 5 Years—Chiang Mai, Thailand

Chiang Mai, Thailand, is a city that has strong potential—the potential for serious real estate profits. I last visited in 2014 and I've been continuing my research on this city ever since.

Unlike the other six locations in this book where you could double your money, Chiang Mai is not a destination I feel I've "conquered." It's not a place where I can give you readymade examples of opportunities where you could double your money. I'm still investigating to identify those opportunities—but I am certain they are there.

Finding the right deals and the right contacts to work with in Chiang Mai is not as easy as it has been in other locales. I'm still working to narrow down my list of contacts there to a trusted, reliable few. The real estate market for foreign buyers is not as well developed or regulated as it is in other countries. And as a foreigner, you cannot hold title to land. (See sidebar on page 89.)

But if you're interested in investing well and potentially doubling your investment, Chiang Mai is well worth your consideration. Big things are coming for this city; if you can get ahead of the trend, you stand to profit.

On my most recent scouting trip here, my first order of business was to track down the smartest local guide I could find. Not someone who's spent the last 20 years showing temples to tourists. I needed someone local, young, and smart.

My brief: Show me Chiang Mai's past, present, and future. We followed arteries in and out of the old city. We visited shopping malls, country clubs, local markets, developers' preconstruction sales offices. I got to see for myself just how this city was starting to grow and develop.

Chiang Mai has long been considered one of northern Thailand's most important cities. You'll often hear it referred to as the "jewel of the north." It's a center of culture, education, and increasingly industry.

But the political turmoil of 2013 and 2014 temporarily put a halt to its growth. Political upheavals stopped the flow of people flocking to this major academic hub.

But it's set to regain its previous status as a major regional player.

Why Chiang Mai?

Chiang Mai has long been a popular place to live—for both Thais and for foreigners.

People come from all over to live there. Besides its own sizable local population—numbering more than 1.7 million for the entire Chiang Mai metropolitan area—expats are increasingly coming. They come from the U.S., Europe, and Australia. Recent estimates put the number of Western expats living in Chiang Mai at around 40,000.

But it's not just Westerners who are moving here. Asian retirees, particularly from Japan, South Korea, and China are coming to spend their retirements in Chiang Mai's relaxing surroundings. And businessmen are relocating, too—including real estate developers priced out of Singapore and Hong Kong.

A Path of Progress is rolling through Chiang Mai, one that has been several years in the making. From a real estate investor's perspective, this current growth stage is interesting. I've followed the Path of Progress and New Middle Class ideas across Vietnam, Cambodia, and

Laos. This is a region at a crossroads of transformation, throwing up a once-in-a-lifetime opportunity.

Northern Thailand's Chiang Mai is set to become an even more important regional commercial, educational, and technology hub. And smart real estate buyers could profit.

The expat demographic is just a small part of what fuels this city—and a small part of the growth story. Chiang Mai has long had a reputation as a center of education. It's a college town, home to about 100,000 students. They study in the universities, language schools, seminaries, colleges, and other institutes of education scattered around Chiang Mai.

Though many of those students are Thai, an increasing number are coming from abroad—especially from China. They're being sent to get a better education than their parents did.

Their story is similar to that of many Americans in times past. First, their parents worked hard to get ahead and to grow their income and status in life. That hard-earned cash gives the next generation every advantage, including an elite education. So those Chinese parents are willing to pay handsomely to give their children advantages they didn't have. They're paying for their children to go to university in Chiang Mai. Some are even moving to Chiang Mai for high school education.

The strong focus on education makes Chiang Mai attractive to global corporations, too. When global corporations look for regional headquarters, they seek out an educated populace to employ. Just like the one on offer in Chiang Mai.

And there's another reason why Chiang Mai is more attractive to global corporations now than in recent decades. 2015 was a momentous year for the 10-country group (including Thailand) of Asean (Association of South East Asian Nations) nations. That's when they rolled out the AEC (Asian Economic Community), a single market designed to encourage free trade among the Asean countries—similar to that of the European Union.

That opens Chiang Mai up to more investment, trade, and new industry. New strategic commercial, manufacturing, and logistics hubs are beginning to emerge. And Chiang Mai, because of its favorable location, quality amenities (including world-class hospitals), and educated populace, is set to benefit.

Already, there's a shortage of high-end rentals in areas close to prestigious hospitals, business parks, and private universities. This is where a real estate investor could do well.

The best way to play this market is to buy a luxury condo preconstruction. Though be advised, it is getting harder to find available condos now with new permitting regulations. You can buy with a few thousand dollars down and manageable monthly payments. I expect capital appreciation during construction. And double-digit rental yields when you take possession of your condo.

I expect you could rent to visiting executives (from Bangkok and elsewhere), folks coming for medical treatments, and wealthy students, both local and foreign.

The prospects for Chiang Mai are strong—a real estate buyer could do well here in capital appreciation and with an attractive rental yield.

How Profit Is Coming as Development Rolls Out

Chiang Mai is readying itself for its transformation. It's working hard to make its potential a reality. It knows what it could be—and it's investing to reach that potential. Trans-border infrastructure has rolled out.

It's already popular with both students and tourists. It has a wealth of universities and training schools. Its historic sites and architectural gems, like 300 Buddhist temples that call Chiang Mai home, attract tourists and scholars. It's also got a very modern side, with high-rise buildings, malls and hospitals, shopping and dining.

Chiang Mai's historic importance developed due to its location on the Ping River and major trading routes. The metropolitan area of Chiang Mai now has a population of over 1.7 million people. Five million visitors come each year; 2 million of these are foreign. Until the 1920s Chiang Mai was only accessible by elephant or by boat. It stayed isolated and distinctive. That changed, of course, as modern infrastructure came. And Chiang Mai's not done growing.

It's got some ambitious plans. These start with a second international airport, capable of handling 17 million passengers.

Then there's a new intercity highway planned. It would run for 114 miles between Chiang Mai and the town of Chiang Rai. This highway would link to the R3A (Asian) highway, which connects northern Thailand with Laos, Myanmar and China. Studies are underway to determine if this project is feasible. If approved, work would begin in 2020 and take five years or so.

More local infrastructure plans include a road linking Chiang Mai to the industrial town of Lamphun, and various ring roads and road widening projects in Chiang Mai itself. There's also talk of a "western gate" to connect this region to Myanmar and India. All these would open Chiang Mai up to increased commerce and industry. Even before all that, its star is on the rise with Thai people.

Increasingly, some Thais are seeing its benefits over the crowded, noisy, frenetic city of Bangkok, where traditionally industry has prospered. Chiang Mai's benefits are tied up with financial and trade route reasons…and some more practical ones, too.

In 2011 Bangkok was hit by a devastating flood. Vast suburbs were submerged. So were many of its sprawling industrial parks. Bangkok's economy ground to a near halt. Major Japanese auto companies saw their global supply chains stall, as products and components couldn't get in or out. Thousands of Bangkok residents were forced to leave their homes. Some for months. Many were drawn north to Chiang Mai.

Who Will Buy in Chiang Mai?

Traditionally, big-town snobbery considered Chiang Mai a sleepy backwater. But now things are different. The high quality of life, great schools and universities, and significantly lower costs of living are increasingly attractive. Many of those displaced by the floods in Bangkok stayed on. Some returned to Bangkok but bought a condo or home here in Chiang Mai and now spend some of their time here.

This flood didn't catch the attention of the Western media; it flashed on and off our TV screens. You might have barely noticed it. But it made Chiang Mai a lot more attractive to people living at lower elevations—particularly in the capital of Bangkok.

The math is simple. Sea levels are rising. Bangkok is sinking. It was creaking under excruciating traffic, congestion, heat and humidity, and poor urban planning even before the flood hit. That makes people consider alternatives. Today many Bangkok residents no longer consider Chiang Mai a backwater. They want to live there. The biggest demand for real estate from outside the province now comes from Bangkok.

The Chinese are also coming in a major way. Middle-class families are coming to set up home and business. But Chiang Mai has more than money-making potential. It's a respite from the congested cities of China and insanely high real estate prices.

Then there are those Western expats I mentioned. They've been coming here for decades, for the warm welcome, rich history and culture, great weather, and a low cost of living.

Japanese and South Korean retirees are also here, and more are on their way. Japanese corporations and manufacturers have had a major presence in Thailand for decades. Many Japanese have worked in Thailand. Demographic changes in Japan are pushing more in this direction. They are coming for the same thing—to escape the winters to the northeast, enjoy space and clean air, and stretch their retirement yen.

University towns like Chiang Mai become hubs for innovation and high-skill jobs. With the removal of barriers between AEC (Asian Economic Community) countries it will be easier for students to come and stay.

Global corporations are looking for footholds with the new economic community—not just to manufacture and ship, but to cater to fast-growing new consumer demands.

Dysfunctional Politics

You may be concerned about the political situation in Thailand. That's not an unreasonable concern. In May 2014, a coup d'état saw a junta take power. Headlines flashed around the world about the situation. Many were concerned for what it might mean for foreigners and the safety of the country.

The truth is: not a lot. A colleague at *International Living* was in Thailand at the time of the coup. Far from serious upheaval or upset, he was almost disappointed to report that life still felt the same as normal. There was no violence in the streets, and no great restrictions on his movements, outside of a brief curfew (from midnight until 4 a.m.) that ran from May to June. As a foreigner, he did not feel in any danger: He was still enjoying his time in Thailand.

And, as I write, there has been political unrest. I'm keeping a close eye on the political situation in Thailand and how it turns out.

Sure, this dysfunction is not great. It would be better if Thailand's politics were more stable. But for an outside investor, they're not currently a major cause for concern. It is the way Thailand's politics have been for a long time. And in fact, there are some signs of improvement.

When I visited in 2014, Thailand's politics were somewhere between dysfunction and on-the-brink. Thailand has a border dispute with Cambodia centered on some temples that leads to gun-fire exchange from time to time. In the south are some Muslim extremists. The jungles across the border in Burma are bandit-riddled.

But, for the right opportunity, Thailand is still a country I would feel comfortable investing in.

Where to Buy

Traditionally Thai people prefer to buy homes on their own plot of land. As prices rise and land becomes scarce they look more toward condos—a trend we have seen in Bangkok. The more mobile will choose a condo as a part-time residence.

As with any place on my beat, I look for opportunities where something big is set to happen. But the opportunity needs to stack up even if the big event fails to materialize or takes longer than expected.

I'm looking for opportunities like fast capital appreciation with a strong rental yield. That opportunity is in Chiang Mai. Right now there's already a shortage of high-end rentals in areas close to prestigious hospitals, business parks, and private universities.

The market I would recommend targeting for rental and resale is the mobile "internationalized" market. This includes visiting executives (from Bangkok and elsewhere), folks coming for medical treatments, and wealthy students. Some of the highest rental rates in parts of Chiang Mai are paid by students. These are children of wealthy Thais, Chinese, Singaporeans, etc. They don't trash their rentals. They come to college to get ahead, not party. They make excellent tenants.

When I visited, a 450-square-foot condo listed for 2,439,500 Thai baht ($75,000 at the exchange rate of the time). This is the sort of purchase I would recommend in Chiang Mai. It's an expensive condo for the local market, but cheap for this internationalized market I'm targeting.

The financing terms were attractive: As a pre-construction property, payments were spread over the one-year build period and finance was available on completion.

You could have rented that condo for 15,000 baht ($430) per month long term. That's a gross yield of 7% yield from the get-go. And I expect rents will continue to rise.

But the developer was more solid than some. He offered contracts in English that were simple, clear, and fair. An appendix to the contract included photos of furnishings and finishes. This was part of the contract. The developer couldn't just swap out cheaper finishes.

That's not par for the course in Thailand. This is a place where you need to tread carefully and do your homework before you make a buy. But buy well in a place like Chiang Mai and you could see strong capital appreciation and a good rental yield as this market continues to develop. As I said, I see potential to double your money in Chiang Mai. I haven't identified the exact development, way, or strategy to do that yet. I'm working on doing just that. In the meantime, this is still a market that deserves your attention.

An Important Note About Owning in Thailand

In Thailand, as in many Asian countries, foreign ownership is not as clear-cut or as simple as it is in Europe and Latin America.

In Thailand, it is important to note that foreigners are prohibited from owning title to land. That's not to say you can't hold land or property in Thailand. You can lease land and homes. Thirty years is the maximum permitted term of such a lease, with an option to renew for another 30 years.

As a foreigner, you can also buy condos (but not a ground-floor condo). But the amount of foreign ownership in a condo building or development cannot exceed 49%.

There is another way you can own. Companies registered in Thailand, with a majority Thai ownership, are permitted to buy land. Foreigners can legally hold a minority stake in such companies.

Lastly, you can own property through a Thai spouse. This is not a route I recommend. The issue there is that you do not own the property—your spouse does. If the marriage breaks down, you may not have any claim to the property.

And beware of snake-oil salesmen offering "easy" solutions. Lots of folks will tell you ways around these restrictions. Some lawyers even peddle solutions. They establish a local entity on your behalf. You are the minority shareholder but retain an option to buy out the silent appointees (nominated by your lawyer) for a nominal amount at any time in the future. Such arrangements are illegal. Let me say strongly: Don't do this! The government is cracking down on this kind of arrangement; and the rights you think you have cleverly secured can be taken away.

If you're thinking of owning in Thailand, make sure to get clear, unbiased advice from a reputable lawyer. And if someone offers you an "easy" way to legally own land, a house, or a condo as a foreign buyer, get a second—or even third—opinion.

CHAPTER 8:

Location #6: Where You Could Potentially Double Your Money in 5 Years—Northern Nicaragua

I'm standing in a meadow dotted with giant ceiba trees, surrounded by horses. The meadow is perched high above the Pacific. The views to the ocean and south along the cliff line are spectacular. Warm breezes rustle the ceiba trees and tall grass.

To the north I can see the coastline of El Salvador and volcanoes of Honduras. This is the end of the road along Nicaragua's Pacific frontier—a truly awesome setting and one that holds incredible values in oceanfront land. This is a location that I see taking off in value in the coming years, as word gets out about its beauty and potential. But for now, you could buy this piece of oceanfront land, which includes this meadow, for $3,000 an acre. That's a buy just as farmland, even without spectacular ocean views.

The seller is quite the pioneer himself. Eloy lives in a wood and tin home with an extended family. Ducks, chickens, and pigs share his yard. His children pose for photos with their pet iguanas. Don't let the basic appearances confuse you, though. He knows a thing or two about following the Path of Progress.

He has bought farms ahead of progress along this coast. Then when progress is close, he sells up and moves his farm farther up the coast, banking serious gains each time. Now he tells us the final stretch of the road is to be upgraded here as part of a tourism initiative.

For me he symbolizes the new Northern Nicaragua: savvy and innovating.

Northern Nicaragua's Transformational Event

It took me a while to catch on to what Northern Nicaragua has to offer. Like a lot of other people, my focus was mainly on the south—on popular beach towns like San Juan del Sur and on the colonial city of Granada.

Tourism development first came to Nicaragua's south—an easy hop from over the border with Costa Rica. Surfers led the way. The south Pacific locales like San Juan del Sur developed as tourism destinations. No one was looking up north.

Up until two years ago, even I hadn't been this far north. There was never a reason for me to visit. But the more time I spent in Nicaragua, the more I realized that big things were coming here. This region, called Chinandega, and the city and province of León below it, is right at the sweet spot of a transformational event. The changes are real and happening.

For a long time, Northern Nicaragua has been largely overlooked by the outside world.

There's no big mystery or story to why. It's been beaten down by war or sentiment. Because of the country's troubled past, Nicaragua had an unfair reputation as a dangerous place. Now that tide is turning. Actually, the UN ranks it as one of the safest countries in Latin America.

The government is focusing hard on increasing the number of visitors to the north. It's already had some success in the south. The Nicaraguan government has been watching its neighbor Costa Rica's success with tourism. It wanted in on that action. So it began to invest heavily in growing tourist numbers and improving infrastructure. Now tourism is the country's second-biggest industry. Tourism numbers have almost tripled in 15 years, from around 580,000 in 2000 to almost 1.4 million in 2015.

And, Northern Nicaragua has it all. You can surf (kite or board), ski on a volcano, moor your yacht in Nicaragua's only full-service marina, or hike in one of the many nature preserves.

But few foreign real estate investors have caught on to the Northern Nicaragua story. That's why you can still buy frontier land with reasonable infrastructure, but with less risk than usually comes from a frontier market.

As part of that drive to increase tourism (and to improve industry in the north), the government is investing in developing Nicaragua's final Pacific frontier. New roads are slated for the area to link up with the country's shiny new highway network.

Industry is set to thrive, as bigger foreign investment comes to the country. That will center on two cities: León and Chinandega.

León is Nicaragua's second city. A new highway means it's now just 75 minutes away from the capital, Managua. León is a colonial, university, and government city. It was the center of power for the Sandinistas in revolutionary times right through to the current day. And the middle class is growing in León. Thanks to more and better industry and the geothermal plant based just outside the city, young professionals have more opportunities than ever before. Where once they used to have to leave home—for the capital city of Managua or to move abroad—greater numbers are staying and finding employment than they have done in the past three decades.

The city of Chinandega is 35 minutes farther north. This is the center of commerce for the north. The region centered on Chinandega was the bread basket of Nicaragua in prosperous times. And it's becoming a prosperous region for agriculture again. Big farming is coming back. And farmland will rise in value as it does.

The Return of the Big Farmer—and How the Market Is Changing

During the revolution, much of the land in Northern Nicaragua was confiscated from the big land owners and big farming families. It was a disastrous move. Productive farms were cut up and given to groups of locals. Production tanked. But over the past decade, the big farmers have come back, bringing their commercial experience and farming expertise.

They have bought back land and come back in times of Sandinista rule. Nicaragua has a long history of disputed land ownership. One side takes and gives to their cronies. The current government welcomes big farmers. And the big foreign energy (geothermal) companies.

Nicaragua's electricity grid has improved beyond all recognition in the past decade, thanks in large part to tapping the endless geothermal resources that bubble and sizzle just underground. The government is moving toward a self-sustaining energy system. They're turning away from costly oil imports. Nicaragua has fertile ground and resources to sustain itself: Some of the world's most abundant reserves of natural energy, like volcanic, solar, and wind, are here.

Today's Sandinistas aren't in the jungles preaching Marx. They are pragmatic businessmen. Sure, they talk a hard, leftist talk to their base. But across the table from international business people, they are helpful and pragmatic.

Over a private, candid dinner, a friend who developed one of the major geothermal plants of the north recounted: "I have nothing but good things to say about the government of Nicaragua."

The Sandinistas know they need electricity and jobs to get re-elected. They need commercial activity to help grow their businesses.

The perception of Northern Nicaragua as backward, dangerous, and unwelcoming to foreign investors persists. Few know that this is rich agricultural country, with vast natural resources and tourism potential.

This place is overlooked because it's misunderstood. It's stunning, relatively developed, and prosperous. There's a smile and a welcome on every face. And it is inexpensive.

Play the Tourist and Middle Class Trends in León to Double Your Investment

The drive from Managua to León is on an excellent new highway. León is a bustling colonial city of more than 200,000 inhabitants. It reminds me of my first visit to Granada down south a decade ago, when the tourists had just started coming.

In León, colonial homes are being renovated. Converted into cafés, trendy sandwich shops, and restaurants. You can see the early stages of a tourist-driven gentrification. But there's more to León than tourists.

Without a single tourist, León is a bustling city in its own right. A center of learning, universities, and government. Proximity to the major geothermal plants means that foreign contractors come here to live. This is a place where we can play much more than just the tourist Path of Progress trend. Nicaragua's new middle class is growing and foreign business people are coming.

You can buy a colonial home here for 30% less than Granada prices. That's a pricing anomaly that reflects where León is on the development curve. Prices for an entry-level colonial fixer-upper start from $60,000.

There's not a lot of competition for vacation-rental colonials. The local owners haven't caught on to the opportunity. With some good marketing and investment in upgrading a colonial, you could be sitting on a nice little earner. You could easily rent out a decent-sized colonial for $1,000 a week. Fill it for 25 weeks (less than half a year), and that's a return of $25,000. Spend, say, $150,000 on a good colonial property (including upgrades), and you could recoup your investment in just six years.

Or you could appeal to that growing middle class and earn handsomely. Own one of the best-in-class homes or condos available, and you're sitting pretty as real estate values rise. And you could collect some strong rental income on top of that. From the get-go, you can comfortably expect to gross at least a 10% return, but that's the starting point on this curve. Rents are likely going to rise as more people can afford homes like this.

In 2016, you could have owned a best-in-class condo in a gated community for $55,000. Now it's completely sold out. I figure you'll double your money on this condo, with a 50% rise in value on your condo in five years and double-digit gross rental yields.

On rental income alone, these condos are returning strong yields. Today, one of those condos rents for $700 a month. That's a whopping gross yield per year of 15%—or 75% in five years.

You can own a condo now for around $65,000. But the sweet spot is to own one of the $80,000 to $90,000 houses offered by one of the first developers to jump on this middle-class trend. Again, on capital appreciation and rental income, you could double your money in five years. I expect you could gross 10% annually by renting one of these condos out. That's a gross profit of 50% on your initial investment on rental income in the first five years.

Prosperous Chinandega: Another Play for Profits

The city of Chinandega is 35 minutes north of León on an excellent road. Chinandega is to commerce what León is to learning. It's a prosperous farm town where everything is clean and tidy. There are malls and grocery stores in the town. Outside town you have a high-end, suburban vibe.

Chinandega's beaches are two hours and 45 minutes from Managua. The Pacific coast south of here, just northwest of Managua, is dry and crisp this time of year. A dry climate and centuries of deforestation means the land has little by way of protection. Not here. In Chinandega, it is lush and green.

Finally the road hits the beach and weaves its way north along the coast. A stunning vista of an empty tan-sand beach opens up. I feel like a pioneer driving a great coast road for the first time. It's empty. I didn't know what to expect. But it wasn't this. Ancient forest rolls down to sea level before giving way to palm trees at the shore. Fishermen bob up and down in their little boats just offshore.

This place looks strangely familiar to me. It reminds me of some of the empty beaches I found in Northeast Brazil and in Las Terrenas in the Dominican Republic. It's nothing like the barren, dry coast immediately south of here. Or the dramatic hills and cliffs of southern Nicaragua. In fact, it's not like any other Pacific locale I know. Down south it's raw and wild. Here is softer and gentler. Elegant.

You don't just have miles of drivable beach. There are beautiful sheltered bays and estuaries. Giant volcanoes tower in the distance. Nicaragua's only full-service marina is nestled in a calm corner of one of the nicest estuaries.

The owner came to the region as a geothermal guy. He had nowhere to berth his yacht so he built a marina and hotel. It's stunning. And secret to all but Nicaragua's boating elite and serious fishermen who come from as far afield as the U.S. for fishing tournaments.

When I last visited in January, Chinandega was beautifully warm and sunny every day. Everything is here. A few short minutes away, and still in the grounds of the marina, a spectacular sandy beach looks across to an empty island.

Right now this stretch of coast is attracting an eclectic group of European and North American pioneers. French and Italians are coming. This eclectic mix of adventure travelers stumbled upon this stunning coastline. They stayed. Surfers came, stayed, and built surf schools. The French came, stayed, and opened restaurants.

Food, health, and wellness are important for these new visitors. They are beginning to attract the high-earning granola set. Surf star Holly Beck has built a home in a little community here and helps to promote it. Another planned community close by is built around a theme of a healthy, active lifestyle.

The developer is building a restaurant at the entrance to the community. Fish will come straight off the boats and vegetables will be grown in the restaurant's gardens. This isn't a locale of seedy expat bars. This is about the outdoors, being active and adventuresome.

A number of gated communities are at various stages of planning and development. I'm currently running the rule over a number of them, but in the early days of a frontier market like this, you need to tread very carefully. Many of the first wave of gated communities will fail.

Right now the best opportunities are outside gated communities. Buy raw beachfront and ocean-view land.

It's important to understand how this location is developing. The folks being attracted to this location are looking for something very special and unique. It's inexpensive here, but the main attraction is this natural wonderland. You won't find any small, cheap, cookie-cutter lots here.

A stunning elevated ocean-view estate lot of three acres, with a drilled well and pump, and electricity to the building site, lists at $85,000. There's a public road right up to the lot. Down the road an empty beach runs north for miles.

Overlooking the beach, with only a little country road separating you from the beach, $89,000 buys you an elevated lot, an acre in size, with long views to the north. Close to the marina, $165,000 buys you a little nine-acre, ocean-view farm. You have stunning views of the flat, blue waters.

In the same area, $155,000 buys an attractive little casita on four-and-a-half acres of stunning ocean view. Some of the land is planted with avocado trees and there's a drilled well. These are the types of values you can lock down in the closest beaches to Chinandega.

As more tourists and expats come, I predict values here will rise. Now is the buying moment.

Sandy Beaches Run for Miles

But outside the already-established tourist locations is where you stand to make the biggest upside. Go farther north and the opportunity is more frontier—and more low cost. As you go north the coastline changes. Long, wide, sandy beaches run for miles. Not snake-like, but in straight lines interrupted only by rocky ridges. Here the land rises to a flat strip. It's typically farmed for growing peanuts today. Historically these were cotton farms.

Behind the flat strip, the land rises steeply, giving excellent ocean views in the distance. You can drive for miles along these beaches. There's very little except agri-business up here. There are some little beachfront *posadas* dotted along the coastline. But access is reasonably good.

Farther north again and the elevations from the ocean are bigger and more dramatic. Some land is farmed for peanuts.

Other land parcels are in pastureland. Pastureland can be bought for less than planted land. Farmland here sells for $3,000 to $5,000 per acre—that's low by international standards for farmland of this quality.

Here's the kicker. You can buy beach- or oceanfront farmland here. This is one of the big ideas I follow: deep value with a kicker for free.

Beach and oceanfront land here comes at a premium of 10% to 60% of what the land would sell for without the views. That's a killer deal. And it's something that's likely to change as more development comes. With a buy like this, you can play both the agricultural trends and the tourism trends. Sit on your land for a few years while development comes, and you could stand to make a killing.

The Smell of a Bad Morning... Or on the Scent of a Killer Deal?

Just before six o'clock in the morning, I sat in the domestic terminal of Managua airport, fueled entirely on coffee and rising irritation. The terminal wasn't any quieter than the hotel room I'd just left. Even at that hour, it was thronged with people—at least one of whom was blasting out local rap music.

I waited to board my plane. And waited. And waited some more. Periodically, a tinny voice came on the intercom to tell us our flight had been delayed. It was 11 a.m. by the time we finally took off.

"Suck it up," I told myself as the plane landed in Bluefields. "Take a deep breath and start again."

Which I did when I exited the plane. I stepped out and filled my nostrils...with one of the worst stinks I've ever had the displeasure of smelling. It didn't go away after I left the terminal. After some investigating, I discovered that the city had just been tree cutting, including one tree—the source of the stench—which is said to be a natural insect repellent. I can tell you, it would double pretty effectively as an unwanted guest repellent. Five minutes of that unholy smell and even the most persistent over-stayer would make excuses to leave.

I wanted to make my excuses to leave Bluefields, even without the smell. I'm going to be blunt here: Bluefields is not my favorite place. I'm told it used to be a charming place, full of Victorian-era wooden buildings, until a hurricane knocked it all down in 1988. Three decades later, it still looks like a hurricane has just blown through. The fact that it's named after a Dutch pirate, who founded it in the 1700s, feels like no coincidence. There's some honest industry. Fishing of the traditional variety is one of its main (and only) industries. Tourism is relatively unknown. But this coast is much more famous for "white lobster" than for its white sands.

"White lobster" is a polite euphemism given to the large bales of cocaine that wash up on the shore in Bluefields from time to time. They end up in the water when Colombian drug runners are trying to outrun authorities. If the authorities get too close, the drug runners dump the evidence overboard. Locals come to stand on the shores of Bluefields every day in hopes of finding that prized catch. They see it as a gift from God. They'll trade it back to the cartel, who'll pay around $4,000 a kilo—a fortune to someone from Bluefields.

I wasn't looking too closely for any "white lobster" as I stood on a marina—a rickety, barely stable collection of planks of rotten wood—waiting for the *panga* driver who'd bring me to my destination. I was hot, achingly tired, and mentally done.

The feeling only intensified after we drove through the muddy and silty bay of the estuary. As we drove, we had to pull into a national guard station. I asked why we had to stop. The man on duty said we had to show our passports and joked (I hope), "If you don't come back, they need to know who you were."

By the time we passed by a post-apocalyptic-looking boat graveyard I was mentally checked out. Like me, it looked like they were in need of being rescued...but they'd been waiting a long time.

But that was when the trip began to change. As we rounded the point of the bay, something wonderful happened. The water became progressively bluer. The land changed from scrubby mud and rock. It was like paradise: azure waters and white sands with palm trees swaying in the background.

The land here is stunning. It makes me think of what Cancún must have felt like in the 1950s. Cancún was less developed than this before the tourism body FONATUR got involved. And even more inaccessible.

Or what Florida's Keys might have looked like before settlers, infrastructure, and even more visitors came.

These days, it's a rare event to stand on almost completely untouched Caribbean sands. Even a small piece of empty beachfront is a big deal. A whole continuous four miles of it up for grabs is an even bigger deal. All for what you could pay for a big closet space in Manhattan.

When you reach the shore, you're standing on virgin, white-sand beach. It stretches for miles. The sun was beating down on my shoulders. I instantly started to relax. It's serene here: quiet, completely unspoiled, and quintessentially Caribbean.

The seller was offering 7,500 acres of land for $1.5 million, down from $3 million. The land includes 3.7 miles of beach and I was told 11 miles of lagoon front. At the north point of the land, you can see some mature trees. There are some little hills and highpoints, but most of it is flat and low.

At first sight, I knew it could be perfect for the right buyer. But the asking price of $1.5 million was too much at that time. The world was in crisis. I knew this would only appeal to a very particular type of buyer. I felt the seller was motivated and so I had negotiation wiggle room. I bided my time. Watched as the seller became more motivated. And finally had an offer of approximately $800,000 accepted, subject to due diligence.

So I made my offer and started due diligence. My advisors went out to investigate the legalities. It looked promising at first: They had a title that looked good. But when my advisors went to the land registry, they found that the page associated with the title had been ripped out from the registry. There was no physical record.

So I backed out. Took my deposit out of escrow and tried to figure out ways to validate the title.

Over time no other titles or owners appeared. The taxes continued to be paid. Only by the guy I was negotiating with. From what I gathered, there were no squatters. No disputes on the title. And the seller still had no buyer.

Another two years passed. I started to think that for the right price this might just be worth a speculative punt.

Given what I knew, there was a risk the title could be challenged down the line. Someone could make a claim, and we would be forced to defend our position. I would only consider taking on a risk like this if what I was buying was insanely cheap—with lottery ticket-type upside.

After another and final low-ball bid a price of $340,000 was settled on for the almost four miles of beach and 7,500 acres. I needed to go back to make a decision on whether I would make this speculative punt—what a friend was now calling "the lottery ticket."

Return to Paradise

I don't know whether it's because I'd gotten better sleep or because I knew the opportunity for this virgin beachfront buy was so much more attractive, but when I returned to Bluefields four years later, I was surprised to find I didn't hate it anymore.

Bluefields felt different. Everything looked a bit prettier. The air was lighter; the temperature was cooler; some places looked like they had a lick of paint.

Even the journey back to see it was easier. At first, I thought history was repeating itself when I arrived to the *panga* dock and was informed that we couldn't use the route I'd used before. A boat carrying tourists on the way to the Corn Islands had capsized in recent weeks. Thirteen Costa Rican tourists had been killed. The authorities had put the open ocean on lockdown.

Instead, though, the driver said we could go by the "*gringa*'s canal." The canal was developed, I was told, by an American lady who cut a channel through a mangrove jungle. For a toll of a couple of dollars, we could use her canal. It was beautiful but slow going. There's a kind of mangrove locals call "iron mangrove." If you press on it, you'd cut your neck open. I was happy for the *panga* driver to take his time. It took us maybe 25 minutes to nudge through.

I was traveling with my contact in Northern Nicaragua, Jordan Clark, and Will Bonner. Will is the son of Bill Bonner, founder of *International Living* and Agora. I often help Bill to find real estate deals with the potential for huge upside, so Will was there to be Bill's eyes and ears.

Bill, based on all my research, was very interested in this opportunity. He was looking for an opportunity for a land-banking real estate investment—something that has massive intrinsic value—beachfront land, for example—but which was currently inaccessible. This land parcel was perfect for that.

In the four years since I'd first seen it, we'd kept this opportunity on our radar. And, as the price kept coming down, its appeal only got better.

The prospects for this land as we saw it were this: You could buy the land really cheaply and either sit on it or develop it in some small way. It would be the perfect place to start a little community for pioneers. But if you were happy to sit on it, this deal could have huge upside.

If the title is good, that is. And the land is developable. And over time this side of Nicaragua improves.

All that said, this lottery ticket comes with a price of just $45.33 per acre—less than the cost of a nice steak dinner per acre.

When Will and I returned to Bill's beach home at Rancho Santana later that day, we sat on the veranda and talked. We were excited.

"So…this looks like a real opportunity," said Bill. "Yep, no doubt about it," I agreed. "If we could buy it…and just hold on…it might come right. Is that the plan?" Bill asked.

"Yep, that's the way it would have to work," I said.

"But of course, that would mean going out there. We'd have to show that we were really in control of it. We'd have to 'exercise dominion' (indicate absolute possession and control) over it, as the lawyers say. So which of you is willing to go there regularly and be in charge of it?" Bill asked.

Will and I looked at each other. I'd been twice. Will had been once. Neither of us wanted to go back. "Well…hmmm…," said Bill. "What kind of paradise is this? Nobody wants to go there."

That was the problem. We just weren't that interested in committing to regular visits to this pioneer territory.

So we passed. It won't be the only opportunity that comes up in Northern Nicaragua. But for someone willing to take a speculative punt, it's an incredible one. The right buyer who has the stomach, vision, and pocket for a punt like this, could be sitting on the next Cancún. All at a buying price of $340,000—or $45.33 per acre.

CHAPTER 9:

Location # 7: Where You Could Potentially Double Your Money in 5 Years—Medellín, Colombia

Forget what you think you know about Medellín, Colombia. Like Nicaragua, it's a place that's known more for an outdated reputation than the reality of Colombia today. To be honest, I don't like to tell too many people that their perception of Medellín is wrong or out of date. Because, while they're still fixated on an image of Colombia and Medellín that's about 20 years out of date, real estate investors who have bothered to get the real story have a chance to get in under true value. Then we'll be sitting pretty as prices rise—ready to watch the value of our investments grow twofold (or more) in the next five years.

The Medellín I know is not the Medellín of *narcos* or the headlines of the '80s. It's a smart, cultured place. The people here are educated and upwardly mobile. They're finding work in one of the major industries that have set up shop here.

When I first put boots on the ground in Medellín in 2011, I was struck by what a bookish place this is. Upper-middle-class condos were packed ceiling high with mahogany book cases. I saw little in the way of pretentious art. Or fads. Just big thick books about philosophy, law, economics. These are the condos of thinking people. Books on Islam and Christianity sit side by side. Books by Marx and Friedman.

Like Northern Nicaragua, this was a place where the young had to emigrate at one time to find work. That's not the case anymore. The diaspora is returning in droves. They're returning home with degrees and letters after their names and money to spend on either owning or renting a comfortable, upscale home.

Word is getting out to the outside world, too. The city's reputation is growing by the year. Today Medellín sits close to the top of worldwide rankings of "most livable cities"—side by side with cities like Barcelona or Copenhagen. It's rated as one of the top three places worldwide for digital nomads to base themselves. These are folks who can live and work from wherever they choose.

A writer friend is one of these mobile people. He's relatively new to Medellín and is only learning Spanish. But he's found it a welcoming and comfortable place to live.

I think these digital nomads are on to something. This is a place where I could live. This is a place I certainly would consider for a winter base. And the real estate story is compelling. There's opportunity to invest well now and watch your investment grow in coming years.

In fact, there's never been a time like now to own in Medellín. It offers one of the strongest opportunities to potentially double your investment on my entire beat.

Medellín's Major Growth Trends

The medium-term prospects for Colombia are strong. After decades of violence, it is relatively stable. A peace deal between government and paramilitaries has just been ratified by Colombia's Congress, as of the time of writing. The signs of industrial progress are all around, too. On my most recent trip, in December 2015, I stayed in the Dann Carlton hotel. I wanted to "look under the hood" of the Medellín opportunity, to talk to my contacts, and to run the rule over ways to play the growing Medellín upper middle class real estate angle. From my research, I knew that the prospects for Medellín were stronger in the medium term than when I first visited in 2011. But on this most recent trip, I got to see the progress it has made since my first trip.

Right across the street from the Dann Carlton, shiny new high-rise office buildings have been completed. There's a lot of new commercial space here. (Maybe too much in the short term.) New tenants are moving in. Big oil. Big banking.

In the past there have been some setbacks for big business. The Medellín-based resource and mining industry was set to take off decades ago. But the resources are in the mountains and valleys all around Medellín. So getting them out was impossible in the bad days. Armed forces of the government, left and right, blew up pipelines or extorted groups out of business. But that's the past.

Now this industry is getting back in business. Contractors are coming to town. So are executives.

Many of the new senior employees will have to be recruited internationally—from the Colombian diaspora in the U.S.; young talent from Spain; and from right across the globe. These folks will all need somewhere to live.

I saw returning immigrants supercharge the economy in Ireland in the late '90s and 2000s. And I expect it to happen in Medellín, too. But even now, the city is vibrant with business and corporate operations.

This is the heartland of learning, professionals, and big commercial conglomerates. On my last visit, while strolling to dinner, I noticed a homeless man curled up and attentively reading the financial pages of a broadsheet newspaper. That summed up Medellín to me. Even the homeless are well read.

The city looks and feels very European. It's also the greenest city on my beat. I'm not talking about a measure of how many people recycle trash or bike to work. I'm talking about trees, bright blooming flowers, gurgling streams that roll down the hillside. It's such a nice city to walk. Rays of sunshine light up broad, verdant leaves. Thick clusters of bamboo trees sit randomly at city street interactions. Open-air gyms are in the shade. Birds chirp, streams gurgle…and sometimes when it rains they roar down the hillside.

The weather is good, too. At 5,000 feet above sea level, it's got a mild climate, with average lows around 62 F and average highs around 82 F. Thanks to that pleasant climate, Medellín is known as "the City of Eternal Spring."

There's more that sets Medellín apart—like the public transport. Public transport in Medellín works. It's mostly safe. And, it's very inexpensive. It's an example of a way of thinking and doing that sets the city apart.

Right across the developing world, poor public transport systems hamper social mobility. Folks living in poor areas can't afford to commute to the areas where they can find work. In some places, a section of society actively blocks connecting their plush locales with poorer areas. Not so here. The metro is held as a symbol of the city. Cable cars link up poorer areas with the main metro lines—an example of Medellín's forward-thinking ways. And big public works are always underway.

Right now the big city project is a "big dig." They are putting a significant portion of the highway that runs through the city underground. The big developers came waving fat check books. They wanted to use space freed up for condos and malls. But the city is using the space left behind for a wide-open park area.

Medellín is fast becoming a hip, "must-visit" city. Livable, internationalized cities like this right across the world are sucking in mobile, creative, and productive people. They generate economic activity. They spawn companies. They need a place to live, fueling demand for real estate.

But Medellín's reputation still reflects the cartel days and its reputation as the murder capital of the world. Real estate values here reflect that reputation. And that's why you can expect to profit—by buying low now before prices rise.

There's another short-term kicker, too. As I write, there's a currency angle at play. Right now your dollar buys you almost twice as many Colombian pesos as it did when I first visited in 2011. Real estate is priced here in the Colombian peso, which has tanked in values over the past two years relative to the dollar.

While that currency is at a low ebb, you can take advantage by buying real estate at low local currency values. The result of that weak currency rate is that you're getting a big discount on already undervalued real estate.

How to Play This Market: Buy in the City's Best Neighborhood

The real estate opportunity is seriously strong right now. If you're looking to increase your investment, you could do far worse than in Medellín. I know of no other world-class city where you can buy a high-end condo of 800 square feet in the city's best address for $120,000.

El Poblado is the best neighborhood in the city. It's on the golden mile. You'll find banks and offices, upscale boutiques, and outdoor eateries, all buzzing with commerce.

Parque Lleras is the main nightlife area and fills at weekends with revelers. This tree-lined park is the focal point of the Zona Rosa, which is the most happening part of town.

I've chosen this area as a base for each of my scouting trips. And this is where you will find the best opportunity.

El Poblado is the most desirable address in Medellín—the place where well-connected locals want to live. It sits in a valley above gurgling streams. This is where the wealthy have lived for decades. It's sophisticated, up-market, and very livable. It is, and will always stay, Medellín's premium address.

The play in Medellín is to buy a completed condo in a nice building a short stroll from El Poblado's amenities and offices. As I write, there's an opportunity to buy El Poblado super-cheap. By buying, you're playing all the angles I told you about above: the currency at a low ebb, compounding real estate prices that reflect an outdated view of Medellín; a growing upper middle-class, including diaspora; and strong medium-term economic prospects. But new regulations have just been implemented that will seriously limit future supply. That's an added sweetener and something that will help to push up prices.

I expect you could double your money on the condo you buy here for $120,000 in the next five years—by targeting double-digit rental income and capital appreciation. And that's being conservative.

But for me, buying bigger is the better investment opportunity. Medellín is a vibrant commercial hub—and by buying a bigger condo, you can cater to professional couples and families who want to live near the action. A five-minute drive away from bank and resource company HQs, in El Poblado, you can lock down a three-bed condo of 2,300 square feet for less than $200,000. This condo is just what the fast-growing number of executives and professionals moving here are looking for.

A Bigger Investment Means Bigger Profits

The best way to play the Medellín situation, if you have budget flexibility, is to spend a bit more. Stretch your budget to up to $200,000, and you could buy a large three-bed condo (about 2,300 square feet). Buy in the best building. It's okay if it's a bit dated. Don't invest in fancy furnishings or finishes. Hold for five to seven years (the length of time I recommend for all real estate investments). The market you're selling to will want to upgrade when they buy.

It's just the type of home professionals and families moving to Medellín will want to rent or own.

It's important to note: You won't get rich by renting long-term. Think of any rental income as the icing on the cake of capital appreciation. Renting long-term, you could charge the equivalent of (in pesos) $1,100 per month for the larger condo. Figure $550 a month for the smaller condo.

But the big play is that you will own something scarce—a condo in Medellín's most affluent and desirable neighborhood. A condo on which I expect you could double your money in five years. One where you can also earn income along the way.

This is a once-in-a-lifetime moment to buy in Medellín. It's a once-in-a-decade moment to buy in a world-class city like this so cheaply.

CHAPTER 10:

The Nuts and Bolts of Buying Well

I'm going to tell you upfront: This isn't going to be the most exciting chapter in this book. After reading about places where you could potentially double your investment overseas, I'm going to bring you back to earth with a bang in this short chapter.

But, while this may not be the most exciting chapter of the book, it is one of the most important—if not *the* most important. The information in this chapter will help you protect yourself against making a bad deal. While the other chapters in this book will help you to make money, this is the chapter that will tell you how to safeguard your money.

The information below forms the principles I use whenever I buy—principles that have helped me to make strong investments, and that have prevented me from investing in questionable or downright dodgy deals.

If you're serious about investing in real estate, this chapter is essential reading.

Your Blueprint for Doing Your Due Diligence

Occasionally, I'll hear about a piece of real estate that sounds like a great deal. The price is low. The property is attractive. And it looks like a buy that could prove profitable.

Sometimes, everything stacks up. The deal is a good one. And the right investor could make a killing.

But, in the world of real estate, a healthy dose of skepticism is a good thing. All that glitters is definitely not gold. It doesn't matter how good a deal a property appears to be. You need to make sure that the deal stacks up.

It's tempting to rush ahead with a deal because the price is low. But there are all sorts of reasons why a piece of real estate might be low-priced. Occasionally, it is because it really is a good deal—the seller has undervalued the property, for example, or because it's in a destination that's on the cusp of a big growth trajectory.

But often, there's a good reason why there's a low price. Maybe because it's not worth any more than what the seller is asking. Maybe there's structural damage that will cost too much for the seller to fix. Maybe there's a toxic waste plant due to be built next door…

The only way you'll know the difference between a genuine, undervalued deal and a piece of real estate that's low priced because it comes with a host of problems is to do your homework.

Avoiding the "Margarita Effect" When Buying Overseas

Doing your homework (also known as doing your due diligence) means thoroughly investigating an opportunity before you make a decision to buy.

This is especially important when you're buying overseas. There's a strange phenomenon I've seen time and time again. Sensible, cautious people take a vacation somewhere exotic. When they're taking an evening stroll on the beach, they see a "For Sale" sign. Suddenly all their common sense goes out the window. There and then, they decide they must have the little house by the beach. This phenomenon happens to otherwise careful people. They don't speak the language. They can't read or understand their contract. And yet they commit to buying a new house in a country they don't know all that well, without ever consulting a lawyer or doing the necessary checks.

Maybe it's the effect of too much sun—or a margarita too many. Whatever it is, it almost always leads to buyer's remorse. And it's not something you should let happen to you.

Buying a piece of property overseas is a serious affair, just like buying back home. Sure, the rules for purchasing may be different, and the way the sale is conducted differs from country to country. But your approach to buying in any country should be the same: measured, educated, and with all your homework done.

At home, you wouldn't trust some guy you met in a bar who tells you his friend has a great deal on some land. It's been in the family for generations, he tells you. The only problem, he says over a cold beer, is that it doesn't have permitting yet so that you can build. But that will be no problem, he promises. It's a quick and easy process. He knows someone who can move the process along…for a fee, of course.

Except after you meet this guy's friend and hand over the cash, you hit problems. Maybe someone else claims the land you've just paid for. Or the permitting process is restrictive, slow, or a complete no-go for new builds.

Reading this, you might wonder who would buy property from a stranger they met in a bar? And without checking title or permitting? The answer: more people than you would think.

You wouldn't spend hundreds of thousands of dollars to buy a place back home without digging deeper into the deal, so why would you act any differently when you're buying overseas, just because a salesman with a glossy brochure tells you it's a good buy?

So what do you do to avoid falling into the trap of the "margarita effect?" Simple. You follow the same tried and true steps you would at home. In case you need a refresher on what those steps are, I've broken it down into a 12-step guide. Copy it down or bring this book with you when you're thinking of buying overseas. Making sure that what you're buying ticks all the boxes on this list could save you hundreds of thousands of dollars.

Your Due Diligence Checklist

Your 12-Step Guide to Due Diligence

1. Hire a local attorney
2. Buy title insurance
3. Check the sale contract
4. Check the title deed
5. Check permits and approvals
6. Check access
7. Check infrastructure essentials
8. Check the developer's background
9. Check the master plan
10. Check the CCRs and HOAs
11. Investigate tax issues and wills
12. Use approved escrow services

These 12 steps are the building blocks of buying well. Let me explain in more detail what's involved.

Step #1: Hire a Good, Local, In-Country Attorney

Using an attorney to vet your deal is good. In fact, it's essential. But it's not a good idea to use your attorney back home when buying overseas.

Sure, you've got a comfort level with the attorney you've used for years. He/she knows you. Knows your personal situation. Right down to the name of your partner, your kids, and your dog.

And your attorney might know a lot about real estate in your part of the world.

What he doesn't know is the legal system or the buying process in other countries. Without country-specific legal knowledge and experience, an attorney can walk you into trouble.

Some legal terms used overseas sound very similar to ones you use back home—but don't mean the same thing.

Additionally, the type of legal system overseas is likely different from the one you're used to. In most of the U.S. and Canada, common law is used. In the world of real estate, common law is very forgiving if you make a mistake or something goes wrong. You argue your case, plead for forgiveness, and reach a compromise with the seller.

Overseas, most countries use civil law. Civil law is much less forgiving. It's very black and white. There's no grey area. You are either right or wrong.

Taking that into consideration, you can see why your home attorney just won't cut it. A different system of law; different clauses and terms; and a different buying process. To make sure you're getting the best legal advice overseas, you need to find a competent in-country attorney.

The way you find an in-country attorney is the same way you find one back home. Look for word-of-mouth recommendations. If you have friends, family, or colleagues who have bought in a certain country, ask them which attorney they used and whether it was a good experience.

Don't just take any recommendation, though. Do not—I repeat—do not use the attorney your broker or a developer recommends. And you should make sure, when you find your attorney, that he or she works only for you. To most of us, that may sound like a given. But it's not a given overseas. In many countries, an attorney can legally represent both sides in a transaction. In their country, it may not be seen as a conflict of interest. So, feasibly, the attorney could be representing you as the buyer, and also the seller, without telling you. Ask your attorney specifically if he/she has any connection with, or represents, the seller.

If you're having trouble finding an attorney with good recommendations, try First American Title Insurance (*www.firstam.com*). The company has a list of approved attorneys it works with in foreign countries. It isn't foolproof, though—I've come across a few bad attorneys that were approved by First American.

Some More Tips

Look for an attorney who is bilingual. You should be able to understand exactly what your attorney is telling you and make sure that he's carrying out your instructions to the letter.

Find an attorney with an interest in real estate or one who regularly handles real estate transactions. He or she is going to be more familiar with local laws, good (and bad) developers, neighborhoods with issues, etc.

Ask your attorney to make sure that every promise the seller has made to you about the property is covered in the contract. Don't just take a seller's word for it.

Ask your attorney to explain any clauses in the contract that you don't understand. Your attorney may not think to explain a clause that is normal procedure in his country—but it may be very different to how you'd do things back home.

That works in the other direction, too. Sometimes you will see a term that looks like one you're familiar with back home. But never assume it means exactly the same thing. Commonly used legal terms can have different meanings from country to country.

I'll go into more depth about sales contracts in Step #3.

Step #2: Buy Title Insurance

If you've purchased in the U.S., especially if you're taking out a bank loan, you purchase title insurance as a normal part of the buying transaction—so why not purchase it for your overseas property? Perhaps because you might not think of it. That's why I've added it to this checklist. The seller or your attorney won't remind you to purchase title insurance.

Occasionally people decide to cut it out to save a few bucks. They reason that their attorney or notary will catch any issues with the title as part of their investigation process. But attorneys and notaries are human. They can make mistakes. Miss something. Or, through no fault of their own, be unaware that someone claiming title to the property will come out of the woodwork five years down the line.

Not buying title insurance could end up being extremely costly for you.

Think of it like this: Title insurance is affordable. Yes, it's an extra expense on top of your purchase, but the peace of mind it gives you is priceless.

What Is Title Insurance and Why Is it Important?

You need to protect any major investment you make. Title insurance is a big part of that.

Title insurance was created to protect a buyer from title claims, liens, and other unforeseen issues that may exist pre-purchase but only become apparent post-purchase. It covers defects in title, property taxes, boundary disputes, hidden defects (fraud, forgery, and unknown heirs)—up to the point when you buy the property.

Title insurance does not cover events (including political risk) that arise *after* you purchase. You are protected up until the point you buy the property. A big caveat here: Anything that you are aware of at the time of purchase is not covered.

Title insurance is available in many countries overseas. You pay a one-off payment upfront and that lasts as long as you (or your heirs) own the property. In the case of a claim, your insurer will cover the defense costs and/or actual loss. If someone challenges your title, based on a past event—forgery of documents, fraud, someone selling a property who was not entitled to do so—then the insurer has a duty to defend that title.

As with any kind of insurance product, not all title insurance policies are equal. Do your research to find the best kind for you. Don't just choose the cheapest option. And check your cover carefully. Make sure you understand what is covered, and what isn't.

Be aware that specific situations may be excluded from your insurance policy. And they may be the very things that are most likely to go wrong. Check exclusions in your title insurance cover carefully, and be aware they vary from country to country.

Title Insurance on Pre-Construction

Title insurance isn't just for constructed properties. If you're thinking of buying pre-construction (sometimes called "off-plan"—more on buying pre-construction in Chapter 12), you need to think about title insurance.

It works slightly differently in the case of pre-construction property. You can get a commitment to title insurance on pre-construction property. That commitment has to be renewed every six months.

Don't rely on the fact that a developer has a master title insurance policy in place. It is a great sign if a developer has one, but it does not cover you; it only covers property he owns. Once the developer has sold you a property—whether that is a lot, a condo, or a home—his insurance cover on that piece of property ends. You need to get individual title insurance when you're ready to buy.

By the way, it's not necessarily a red flag if a developer doesn't have a master title insurance policy, but you should always ask why. Sometimes the answer is simple: He may be dealing with local buyers, who don't ask for title insurance. Or the developer may never have even heard of title insurance—not unusual in some countries.

But occasionally, there could be more sinister reasons, so it is worthwhile checking.

Step #3: Check the Sale Contract

One of the most important parts of this checklist is your sale contract. This document outlines exactly what you're buying in black and white. Ensuring that you understand your contract is essential. If you don't understand what you're buying, or you're not happy with any part of it, don't sign the sale contract. Trying to renegotiate after you have signed that contract is pointless. Once you've signed, you're legally committed to what's in the document.

Make sure that the contract you're reading is the legally binding version. Sometimes a developer or seller will give you a sale contract or purchase agreement in English. That's a nice courtesy but it may not be the binding contract. Only a contract that is in the official language of the country that you are buying in is legally binding, whether that is Spanish or Portuguese or French. If you have a dispute with the seller, if you need to go to court, then the contract in the language of the country will be the one that you use.

Have your attorney translate the sale contract for you. Ask your attorney to explain any clauses or terms that you are not sure of.

Here are some major ones to look out for:

- **Check that the property details, description, and price are correct.**
- **Check that the seller's name matches the name on the current title deed.**

- **Ask your attorney to check that your sale contract/purchase agreement gives you title, free and clear, on closing.**

  That may seem obvious but sometimes contracts don't give you title on closing. I've seen a few that give you possession of a condo, and the keys, but not the actual registered title. Instead, the developer simply stated that he would register it at some point (with an undefined time period). Have a specific timeframe in the contract for you to get your title deed—and hold money back until that happens.

  I've also seen a few contracts that gave title but did not include a mechanism for the seller paying off his mortgage related to the property. The mortgage stays with the property in most countries overseas. For that reason, if a seller has a mortgage, have him pay if off in full before the property title transfers to you. Also make sure that there are no outstanding taxes, fines, HOA fees, water rates or liens on the property.

- **Check for any unfair penalty clauses in your contract.**

  Sellers like to incorporate penalty clauses into your contract. It's normal overseas that once you sign the contract, if you default for any reason you will lose the property and whatever monies you have paid to date. I have seen contracts where they not only keep the property and the money, but make you pay the full purchase price—and sometimes add a fine on top.

  Penalty clauses should work the other way, too. Ask what happens if the seller defaults (say, by not transferring title to the property to you within the agreed timeframe). You should ask for all penalties to be reciprocal.

- **Check any price adjustments.**

  These apply to pre-construction property. In some countries, such as Brazil, Costa Rica, Panama and Mexico, for example, developers have a clause stating that if construction costs rise during the build period, they can charge an additional fee, based on a percentage of the property's purchase price. That percentage can be as high as 10%. So, in that case, if you agreed a purchase price of $100,000 for your condo, you could end up paying $110,000.

The additional fee is payable on closing in many countries. Developers are supposed to prove that construction costs have actually risen, using government figures and statistics. In Brazil, the adjustment is monthly, if you are making monthly payments to the developer during the construction period.

Step #4: Check the Title Deed

Having title insurance does not negate the need to do a strong and thorough title check. Your attorney will handle this.

In some countries the registry is online. In others, the attorney will have to search through physical documents to check the title. In some cases, your attorney will need to use a notary public to check the documents.

From that title check, your attorney should be able to tell you the current registered owner and value, the boundaries, previous sales and transfers, whether there are any liens or mortgages or taxes outstanding on the property, and if there are any annotations such as rights of way, etc.

Some things that you should have your attorney check when investigating title:

- **Make sure that your seller is the property owner.** This is an obvious one, but important. Make sure the person you're buying from has the right to sell the property.
- **Check if your title is registered or possessory.** In some countries, they can seem similar. You can live in a Rights of Possession property, record your claim to it, and you can sell

it. There is a difference, however. Registered title means you own the land. Possession means you have the right to occupy the property, until someone with a better claim to it turns up. When they do, you may lose the property and the money that you paid for it. I recommend that you only purchase freehold, titled, fee-simple property.

- **Check the title chain.** Be careful if there's a record of *co-operativa* (shared ownership) or confiscation. Similarly, in Mexico, if land was formerly *ejido* (indigenous-owned) land, tread carefully. Both issues can be a potential landmine, as they could indicate that someone may lay claim to your property in the future. In these instances, your attorney will have to do extra checks to make sure that the title is clear, and all transfers were done correctly.

- **Make sure you can own that piece of beachfront.** The right piece of beachfront land may sound like a great buy. But be careful that you can actually own it. Most countries overseas have a section of the beach related to the high-water mark where you cannot legally own a property.

  That caution doesn't just apply to owning beachfront land. I've come across cases of people buying beachfront condos, just meters from the water. The only problem was that it was illegal to build or own residential property there.

- **Check if you can legally own as a foreigner.** Occasionally you, as a foreign buyer, will be barred from purchasing what a local can buy. Foreign buyers are usually not allowed to own property close to a country's international borders. The distances for these zones are not standardized, but vary from country to country, so be sure to double-check what that distance is if you are planning on buying near the border.

  Foreigners may face restrictions, too, on Caribbean islands for example. They may not be able to buy investment property (where they rent the property out rather than keeping it for personal use), or they have to purchase a property in certain areas or of a certain value.

In some countries, too, particularly in Asia, foreigners cannot legally own property outright. There are ways around this, but ask your attorney to investigate thoroughly.

Step #5: Check the Permits and Approvals

Never take a seller's or developer's word that all the necessary permits are in place. I don't care if they seem to be the most trustworthy individual. It doesn't matter if they're a respected businessman, someone with political connections, or a billionaire. A verbal contract about permitting isn't worth anything. Get your attorney to check that all the promised permits are in place.

If a developer is open with you that they are waiting on a permit or two, that is not necessarily a black mark against him/her. In many countries, patience is a must-have when it comes to permits. The process can move a lot slower than it does in the U.S.—and in some countries, there are far more bureaucratic hurdles to get through before a permit will be granted.

There are a number of necessary permits to get in any development. The standard ones are environmental, water, construction, and municipal permits.

(By the way, if you're buying land with a view to developing it, you need to be even more familiar with the country's permitting requirements and processes. You need to know how long the process takes, how much it costs, and what you will need to do to comply with regulations.)

Have your in-country attorney check to make sure that your seller/developer has all the permits and approvals he needs to comply with current regulations.

Find out if the developer you're buying from has the necessary preliminary approvals or permits in place. Many countries require projects to have developmental and environmental pre-approval before they can be legally marketed or sold. That process can take up to two years, and until pre-approval is granted, the developer cannot start selling—or construction.

If you're in a country that bans marketing and selling before that pre-approval is granted, and a developer is selling without it, take that as a red flag. If a developer hasn't done things correctly at that early stage, it could be a sign that there will be problems further down the track.

But the lack of a particular permit doesn't always mean a developer is crooked. As I said, permitting processes can be slow in a lot of countries. If you're buying abroad, you need to be aware of that. If you're offered the chance to buy in a development that has all but one final permit granted, you may decide it's worth the investment and go ahead, anyway.

That's fine. In most cases, that permit is likely to come through. And then you'll be sitting pretty with your new buy. But never take it as a given. And make sure you protect yourself in that situation.

If you find yourself in a situation where you want to buy but the developer is waiting for one last permit, tell him that you're putting your money (whether it's a deposit or the full purchase price) in escrow until the permit is granted. That way, you're protected should the permit not be granted—and you won't have to fight to get your money back.

If you do put your money into escrow, use an approved escrow service with an established company, like First American Title Insurance.

One More Note About Permitting

Permitting issues don't just apply to pre-construction properties. Just because something is move-in ready doesn't mean it has all the necessary permits.

In some countries, you can see houses for sale that have either never applied for planning approval, or had initial approval but subsequently added an extra unapproved bedroom or garage. This is particularly true in rural areas. It can lead to problems, if the authorities fine you or order the home to be demolished. Have your attorney check for you, and ideally get the seller to legalize the property before you buy it.

Step # 6: Check Access

Never assume that you have automatic access to the property that you are buying. The broker/seller might have taken you on a certain road to view a property. But that doesn't mean he has permission to.

If access to the property is via a right-of-way through someone else's property, that needs to be stated in the deed.

And don't assume only you have the right of way through your property. Have your attorney check this for you, and ask neighbors and locals if anyone has been using your property as a right of way for any time period.

Step #7: Check Infrastructure Essentials

No matter what you're planning to do after you buy a property overseas, you need to make sure you're comfortable with the infrastructure in place. That applies whether you plan to live in it yourself, rent it out, or develop a piece of land.

Infrastructure may be way down your list when you're thinking of buying property. But in the long run, the infrastructure—or lack thereof—can have a big effect on how comfortable or hassle-free your purchase is, and how valuable the property is.

You may be willing to buy initially without some of the essential infrastructure in place for the sake of a good deal. The lack of infrastructure might not be a deal breaker in that scenario.

But you should always ask the questions below before you buy.

Water:

- Is there a source of potable water on the property?
- What's the water pressure?
- What's the purity?
- If there isn't a mains supply, who will drill a well? If it is you, can you get a permit to do that, and if so, how deep will you have to drill—and how much will that cost?
- How is waste treatment being handled? And does it comply with local regulations?
- Will there be a municipal system, a system put in place by the developer, or will you need to put in a septic tank?
- If a septic tank needs to be installed, check local regulations to see how much you will have to spend? (Some environmentally sensitive areas require a very high-tech, and very expensive, tank.)

Electricity:

- Is it in place, and if not, what timeframe (and cost) are you looking at?
- Is it reliable, or will you need a back-up generator?

Roads:

- Are roads and pavements already in place?
- If not, when will they be, and what standard will they be? Remember, developers often leave roads until last, as road surfaces can be damaged by heavy construction equipment.

Internet

It might seem less essential than roads, water, or power, but if high-speed internet is an absolute necessity for your job or your business, check that it is available in your area (preferably by contacting a service provider). Ask what the speed is in MB (megabytes) and how much it will cost. Ask locals about its reliability. High speed or broadband internet in some countries I have visited is at a snail's speed. In some destinations, internet services can cut out for large portions of the day. Can your business or job survive outages like that?

How to Protect Yourself

Ensuring that you get what you were promised goes back to your sale contract. You can try to cover yourself by ensuring that your contract has firm timelines, standards, and commitments for the essentials. And when you're buying pre-construction, never pay in full for the property. Hold money back until you get what you were promised in the contract. You can add a clause to the contract that states specifically that you are holding back, say, 15% of the purchase price until you get whatever you are being promised (roads, electricity, water, the fancy gourmet kitchen, the clubhouse and swimming pool).

Step #8: Check the Developer's Background

If you've read this far, I'm assuming that you're smart and sensible. So I'm going to make some assumptions about how you'd act in certain situations. Specifically, how you spend your money.

I'm assuming that you'd never do any of these things...

You wouldn't send money every month to a guy off the street just because he said he was a banker. You'd never start a business with some woman you'd never met before because she sent you a flyer that said you'd get rich. You wouldn't buy a flashy sports car without taking it for a test drive.

So why would you hand over hundreds of thousands of dollars to someone you don't know? When you put it like that, it sounds obvious. But people do. They see a nice brochure or get the grand tour from a charming sales guy. And they put their trust in someone they know nothing about.

Sounds crazy, right? It is. And it's not something you're going to let happen to you.

Making an investment in real estate is a business transaction—whether you're buying the property for personal use or to make a profit.

Before you even think of handing money over to a developer, make sure you know as much information as you can about that developer and her track record.

Here's a list of questions and pieces of information you should find out:

What is the developer's track record?

Knowing a developer's track record can give you some idea of the probability of success of his development. Find out whether your developer has finished a project before. A developer with no proven track record to his name isn't necessarily a bad thing. Still, you're taking a greater risk with an unproven entity. Ask yourself if that risk is worth it.

If the developer has completed a project, ask where it is and when it was constructed. If you have the time and the funds, visiting one of the developer's finished projects could give you an indication of the quality of his past work. That's not a guarantee that the current development will be of the same quality, but it can give you an insight into what his standards are.

How happy are past and current customers?

Ask the developer upfront if he can provide you with written testimonials from previous buyers. If he has dozens of testimonials from happy buyers, that's encouraging. And get some email addresses from buyers you can contact to verify that they are indeed happy with their purchase.

In addition to requesting testimonials and emails from the developer, do your own digging. If you have an opportunity to talk to previous buyers (whether at any previous project or the developer's latest one), take it. Ask them for their honest opinion about their experience.

How is the developer financed?

Knowing your developer's solvency is a must. You never want to put yourself into a situation where a developer starts a project you've bought in and then runs out of money before completing it.

To be clear, buying pre-construction is always a risk. There's no way to protect yourself 100% against that risk. By buying pre-construction, you're taking a risk that a project will be completed as promised. But pricing for pre-construction property is generally lower than buying a finished property. The trade-off for that lower pricing is accepting the risk.

That said, there are ways you can ensure your chosen developer is as robust as possible. To do that, you have to dig deeper into the developer's finances.

First, you need to find out how the developer is financed. (You do that by asking the developer and checking the title of the project, which your attorney can do.) Does he have loans or mortgages on this development or any other? If so, how is he proposing to pay them off? If he is committed to repaying those before he starts construction, that is not ideal: You'll likely wait a long time before your home is built.

If he needs money from sales to finance the project, how likely is he to achieve the sales level he needs in the current market? Bank financing often kicks in when a developer has a certain amount of inventory sold. That percentage could be anywhere from 20% to 80% of the project being sold. A bank will give a developer financing based on a number of factors, including the developer's track record and the market he is operating in. Banks are becoming more cautious since the economic downturn, and tightening lending restrictions. Why is this important to know? Because if you're one of the first buyers, it's preferable for you if the developer starts construction when he is 20% sold rather than 80%.

Who's building the project?

Some developers have their own team for construction. The majority, though, do not. Usually a developer will hire a construction company to build his project. If that's the case, you should find out about the construction company. What is their background and track record? Can you see some of their finished projects to confirm whether you are happy with the quality of their work?

And you need to find out if the developer has insurance that covers him in the event that his constructor goes bankrupt or can't complete the work or fails to complete it satisfactorily.

Insurance means a delay while the developer waits for the funds to restart construction, but it's better than the alternative of a half-finished project.

Step #9: Check the Master Plan

I'm starting to sound like a broken record, but it bears repeating and often: If you are promised something by anyone—whether that is a real estate agent, broker, seller, or developer—get it in writing.

When it comes to pre-construction, you should take that advice and apply it to what's promised in the master plan.

A master plan is the plan a developer puts together for a whole project. It will show amenities like swimming pools, clubhouses, barbecue areas, tennis courts, and landscaping. When it's on the plan, it's only a promise. And promises can easily be broken. A contract is much harder to break.

If you can, get the developer to put in writing in your contract details of the promised amenities. That should include, where possible, standards, sizes, and timelines for completion. Otherwise, don't be surprised when that massive pool with a giant water slide that you were promised ends up being a kiddies' paddling pool.

Amenities are usually the last items installed in developments, and the first that suffer if a developer is running short of cash.

You should also ask questions about any reserve areas or green spaces on the masterplan. Just because it's a green area now doesn't mean the developer hasn't earmarked it for something else at a later date. Ask whether the green spaces or reserve areas will be preserved or used for future development. Similarly, if there's empty land next to the property, find out what plans are in place for it. You don't want to wake up one day to discover a new factory is being built beside your new condo.

Check the local municipal developmental and zoning plan, if there is one, to see if roads or factories are planned nearby. Similarly, check out the local area to see if there's anything that might disturb your enjoyment of your new property. Is there a municipal dump close by, for example, or a truck park, close to your new home?

Step #10: Check the CCRs/HOAs

Homeowners Associations (HOAs) apply when you purchase a condo or a home in a gated community. They enforce the rules and regulations of the community.

HOAs typically outline their rules in the Covenants, Conditions, and Restrictions (CCRs for short). The breadth and depth of CCRs differs from one HOA to another. Make sure there is nothing in the CCRs that you can't live with. Some are relatively easygoing; others are mapped out with military precision and enforcement.

CCRs can cover what kind of pets, if any, you can keep. Some have restrictions on working from home; if you intend to work from home, find out what those restrictions are.

Some set out standards for maintenance—including how often you have to carry out work and how it should be completed. CCRs can dictate down to the smallest detail how you should maintain your home—right down to the color you can paint your house or what you can plant in your garden. (I've heard of one recently that even dictated what direction a car could be parked in. Front bumper to curb was fine, apparently. Trunk side to curb would get you a stern warning from the HOA.)

Of course, those restrictions can work in your favor, too. If you're not happy that your neighbor has painted his house purple or that he bought a rooster for his yard that wakes you up at 4 a.m. every day, the CCRs could be your best friend. The rules of a CCR should be loose enough that you can enjoy your home, but tight enough that your neighbor can't decide to start an all-night club next door.

If you're thinking of subleasing your property for vacation rentals, find out if you're allowed to do so before you buy. There's no point investing in a property to earn rental income only to find that short-term rentals are strictly prohibited.

What do your HOA fees pay for?

I like to golf. I golf whenever I can. That's why it makes sense for someone like me to buy a home that sits right next to a golf course.

Non-golfers sometimes choose to buy in a golf community. They do it for a variety of reasons. Some appreciate the quiet, manicured green space on their doorstep. Others might want to rent their home out, and a golf course is an added attraction for many renters. If the golf course is a completely separate business they're not paying for, they get all the upside of golf course proximity with none of the expense of a golf club membership.

But if you're a non-golfer, you might want to think carefully about buying in a golf community, even if you're told at the beginning that you don't have to pay. A recent court case highlights why caution is advisable.

In a California community, the community's homeowners association (HOA) is now footing the shortfall after the community's golf course got into trouble. At the time of writing, some of the homeowners affected were suing the HOA.

The community's HOA asked owners how they felt about supporting the struggling golf course in their community. A narrow majority (63% of the 94% of owners who voted) agreed to support the golf course. So the HOA tacked on $250 a month to the $1,050-a-month dues each owner already paid, just to support the golf club.

That wasn't so bad for the golfers who owned a home in the community. Golf club members got a $250 monthly credit on their membership that offset the additional charge. Owners who were not golfers felt they were carrying the burden. A group of those non-golfing owners launched a lawsuit against the HOA.

You could argue that keeping the golf course in good shape is in everyone's interest. A badly maintained, un-watered course, or one that's closed, can negatively impact property values. But the question remains, who should pay if the golf course can't fund itself? Or what happens if it goes bankrupt?

This is something you need to consider when you're buying in a community with an amenity such as a golf course or equestrian center or wellness center. Even if you're not using the amenities right now, and it's a free bonus that bumps up the value of your home, how would you feel if you were asked to pay toward it in the future? If it's a deal-breaker, you might want to consider buying a home in a community with few or no shared amenities—or ensure you have enough disposable income to foot increased HOA dues at some point down the line.

How the HOA is run and managed

Besides CCRs, there are some other things you should know about the HOA. First up is how it is managed and financed.

Know exactly who will manage the HOA (Homeowners Association) initially. If it is the developer, find out when the handover to owners happens.

Then you need to find out what the projected monthly dues are. Are they likely to change? And can the HOA legally enforce collection? If not, those lovely shared amenities could deteriorate very quickly. If other owners are refusing to pay—and the HOA can't force them to—who's going to pay to keep the road surfaces in good condition or the elevator in working order?

But there's another question to ask: Who is or will be managing the HOA finances—and are there checks and balances in place to ensure that funds are managed correctly?

Find out if there is a reserve fund set up. Ideally, you should make at least two extra monthly payments a year that should go into a reserve fund, just in case any serious, costly maintenance issues come up. Many owners ditch the reserve fund to cut their monthly bill. Then when a big-ticket expense crops up, there's no money to fund it, and many owners will refuse to pay, even if it's an essential, like urgent repairs to the roof of a condo building.

Last thing to consider: Are the CCRs and HOAs tied into the property deed? Are they enforceable against future owners if the current owner sells? Don't assume that because CCRs are in your deed that they are enforceable. They must also be set up under a proper statutory regime that varies country by country. Your attorney can check this for you.

A Cautionary HOA Tale

If you're buying somewhere that has a Homeowners Association (HOA), you need to be sure you know exactly what your obligations are. The cost of not knowing can be high.

HOAs are typically found in private or gated communities. They're the bodies that enforce the rules and regulations of the condos or houses in those communities. They also set the monthly fees every owner must pay to cover the cost of maintenance and repair of shared amenities like roads, elevators, and swimming pools.

The monthly fees are a bone of contention for many owners. More so when you're buying pre-construction. It's often hard to get a handle on how much you'll pay per month. Plus, while the community is under construction, the developer normally runs the HOA until most of the homes are sold, when control passes to the owners. Owners don't always agree with the developer's decisions and price-setting. But there's no guarantee that things will go any better once the owners take charge.

Some owners think the easiest solution when they're at odds with the HOA or they're cash-strapped is to simply stop paying their monthly fees.

But, as one owner in Texas recently discovered, that can lead to all kinds of problems—such as losing your home.

The homeowner was busy setting up a new business. Her HOA fees slipped through the cracks. She racked up $1,800 in unpaid HOA fees. The HOA ultimately sold her home at auction to recover the fees. The owner hadn't missed any mortgage payments, by the way. The foreclosure and sale by auction related only to the $1,800 of unpaid HOA fees.

The owner didn't understand the consequences of not paying the fees. She certainly had no idea it could lead to her losing her home.

My tip when you're buying in a condo block or gated community is to do your research. Ask lots of questions about who will run the HOA, how board members are elected, and how decisions are made and implemented. Find out how much you'll pay per month in HOA fees and how that money is spent. Investigate what happens if you're late paying or can't pay the fees. And make sure there's a reserve fund. Extra cash from HOA fees should go to the reserve fund, to pay for big-ticket expenses like replacing an elevator. If you're buying pre-construction and the HOA rules have not been set up, ask the developer (in writing) what rules he plans to implement, how the HOA will be run, and an approximate level for monthly fees.

Step #11: Investigate Tax Issues and Wills

As Benjamin Franklin once wrote, there is nothing certain in life but death and taxes. It's not pleasant, but you have to consider both when you're buying property overseas.

To start with the arguably less unpleasant of the two (though opinions on that one vary), you should get an idea of your tax obligations before you buy property overseas.

Your attorney or a good CPA/financial adviser with foreign real estate experience can discuss with you the best way to hold your property overseas. This is a very personal matter that depends on why you're buying the property, what you plan to use it for, and your current tax circumstances.

The other thing you need to consider is what happens to you in case of your death. You may need to have two wills, one in the country you are buying in, and one back home. If you are a couple, how would the death of one partner affect the property ownership?

Make sure to get good advice from both your in-country attorney and your tax advisor back home.

Step #12: Use Approved Escrow Services

Before you start making payments to the seller, you should consider escrow services. Escrow is the best way to protect your money when you're buying overseas.

You should never pay the seller directly. Nor should you send the money to your real estate agent or attorney in-country. They may not have a separate client account—and there are likely no protections or insurances if they decide to take your money and run.

You should use an approved escrow service. That way, your money is protected and only released to the seller when certain conditions are met—getting the final permit, finishing construction, title transferring to your name, etc.

To Sum Up

The rush of negotiating a price, and the satisfaction of locking down a property you want, are incredible. The point of this chapter is to make sure that those emotions won't override your good sense. It's to ensure that when you get the property you want, you can enjoy it without the worry of any unexpected pitfalls.

Follow the steps above and use them to buy wisely and safely overseas.

CHAPTER 11:

3 Strategies for Doubling Your Money

There's an old adage in real estate circles that goes, "You make your money buying." It's a saying that's served me well.

The idea is that you buy property knowing where your profit is going to come from. Whenever I invest my money in a piece of real estate, I do it based on fact and educated decision-making. I do my homework, run the numbers, and have a clear picture of the potential profitability of my purchase before I go ahead with the deal.

That's what sets a real estate investor apart from a real estate buyer. Being a successful investor does not necessarily come from having a big portfolio of real estate. That, in and of itself, doesn't indicate the profitability of those purchases. Let's pretend you're a jet-setting billionaire with fun money to spend. You decide to buy 20 different properties just because you can. You pick the properties because you like the style of the home or the interior design. Or they're in a cool city or on a tropical island you like to visit.

Without a clear strategy in mind when you're buying, those 20 different properties—no matter how nice or luxurious—might never appreciate in value. When it comes time to sell, you might find you struggle to get back what you paid. You might even make a loss.

If you're buying just for the sake of buying something nice, and because you have the spare cash, have fun! There's a lot of gorgeous real estate in the world that you can have your pick of. Enjoy it.

But if you're reading this book with a view to becoming a real estate investor—or just to make sure you buy well—that attitude won't cut it.

You need to have a clear picture of the profitability of your chosen piece of real estate when you buy. If you can't sum up quickly where your profit is going to come from, you haven't done your homework properly.

It doesn't matter what you're buying—or why. You may be an investor in multiple properties. Or you may just want to own a second property for personal or rental use. My advice is the same either way. It doesn't matter what the scale of your investment is. If you're expecting to make money on your purchase, you need to go in, eyes open, with a clear understanding of where your profit is coming from. It's too late after you've purchased to try to figure out how you can monetize your purchase. The time to figure out where your profit will come from is before you sign on the dotted line.

This chapter will introduce you to the best and most profitable strategies I've found.

Where and How to Spot a Killer Deal

There's no single way to make money on real estate. You'll hear some real estate "experts" tell you that there is one magic formula that "guarantees" real estate profits. I'm not going to do that. For one thing, it's just not true. Steer clear of anyone who tells you otherwise.

Sure, some investors have their favored strategies—ways of buying that have served them well previously and that they have profited from. That may work for them, and it's a legitimate way of identifying real estate opportunities. Some people can carve out a strong niche for themselves identifying a single real estate investment strategy that works for them. You might, too. You may find that utilizing just one of the strategies I discuss in this chapter works best for you.

But personally, I don't just chase one real estate niche to identify profits. That would limit the opportunities available to me and to members of my *Real Estate Trend Alert* group. Instead, I have a number of strategies and methods for identifying strong real estate opportunities. Some of those strategies I've touched on in previous chapters. I'll explain more about them in this chapter.

The strategies discussed will help you to identify paths to profiting from real estate—including how to buy under market value or where prices are set to rise. This isn't an exhaustive list. A complete list could fill this book three times over. But these are among the strongest strategies I utilize—and ones you can use for yourself.

In Chapter 13, I'll give you the lowdown on owning real estate to rent out—how to spot a strong rental market and how to capitalize on your buy to command the strongest possible rental yields.

To start with, let's talk about the different ways you can buy real estate at killer pricing that's set to rise in value.

#1: Crisis Investing

One of the best and most obvious ways to profit from the get-go in real estate is to find and buy something that's undervalued. When you can lock down a big savings on a piece of real estate at the time you purchase, you're already ahead of the game.

One of the best ways to do that is crisis investment. That means you buy when a market is experiencing difficulties. Then profit when things recover.

It's a concept that's been around for centuries. It's something the nobleman and member of a major banking family, Baron Rothschild, described in the 18th century when he's said to have coined the adage, "Buy when there's blood in the streets."

That saying has influenced contrarian investors ever since.

The thinking behind Baron Rothschild's statement is that a crisis is the time to snap up an asset cheaply. Then, when the crisis is over, you have an asset that's worth many times more than you paid. That's the thinking, anyway. In practice, a move like that can be a gamble. Sometimes it pays off big, if you know what you are doing. But sometimes it's a wasted investment.

Not every crisis offers an opportunity—especially not for savvy real estate investors. Identifying the crises that offer opportunity takes research and an understanding of global markets. It's not as easy as seeing a crisis and acting—rushing in to snap property up at low pricing, and hoping it will rise in value.

The truth of the matter is that there's always crisis somewhere. Check *CNN* now and you can probably identify a dozen countries or economies in crisis.

Take Venezuela, for example. I've been keeping a close eye on it and watching how its current economic crisis is playing out. But, having watchfully waited, done my research, and analyzed its chances of recovery, I haven't moved. I haven't recommended anything. I won't do so unless or until there's some clear path to profit. For the near future, I don't think there will be. But I'll keep waiting and watching to see if opportunity arises.

Some crises take a while to play out. For others, there's no end in sight. Take Argentina. Every so often a reader writes to ask if Argentina is worth investing in. And every time, my answer is "no." I've kept a close eye on Argentina for years. It's a country that's perpetually in crisis. There's no sign of its stabilizing any time soon. So I won't be making a recommendation there, either, for the foreseeable future.

All this may have given you the impression that I'm not keen on crisis investing. That's not the case. Crisis investing can be one of the strongest strategies in your arsenal for buying low and profiting in the medium- to long-term. You just have to know what you're doing.

Where the Crisis Angle Works

For a crisis to be an opportunity, two things need to be in place. You have to be able to get real estate for cents on the dollar—and you have to see a clear end to the crisis and the prospects of a bounce back in the future.

That's how I, and readers of my *Real Estate Trend Alert* group, have done so well in Spain and Ireland in recent years.

As I told you in Chapters 5 and 6, Spain and Ireland are both markets where a real estate investor could have potentially doubled his money in recent years.

Both countries were hit by severe economic recessions. They were two of the countries hit hardest by the recession that ripped through Europe from 2008. It's hard to describe how tough a time both countries had it. Unemployment spiraled—youth unemployment, particularly. Many of the best and brightest emigrated to more prosperous shores. Many people defaulted on mortgages. Developers went under. Their governments struggled to cope and to reverse the dramatic downturns.

I advised members of my *Real Estate Trend Alert* group to bide their time. Because it takes time for the right moment to show itself in the wake of a crisis. Move too fast and you'll pay over the odds for real estate that is still falling in value. Wait too long and you'll end up paying more as the market recovers. You need to find the sweet spot in the middle—where prices have bottomed out before recovery comes.

It took three years of watchful waiting for me to recommend moving on Ireland's crisis. That was when the country's new "bad bank," NAMA, launched its first fire-sale auctions. Until that moment, there had been mass denial about the state of the real estate market. Sellers were still hoping their inflated asking prices would be met. When fire-sale auctions came, it laid bare the country's true market values. Sellers could no longer hide behind what they hoped their property was worth.

For the first time since the start of the recession, they were forced to face reality.

That brought prices crashing down—and gave real estate investors their moment to act.

Something similar happened in Spain. Right down to the bad bank's getting involved. It was in 2013 when SAREB, Spain's "bad bank," started selling off the properties on its books.

If you had gotten in on Spain and Ireland's crises at those buying moments, you could have done seriously well. Recommendations I made at both times have increased by up to 60%, as both countries' economies improve.

You don't always need a crisis to benefit from crisis-level pricing. Not every market that was once in crisis sees as quick or strong a rebound as Ireland and Spain have. Sometimes the reputation of a crisis is enough to depress prices long after a crisis abates. That's what's happened in Medellín, Colombia. Today, Medellín is still living in the shadow of its past. That means its pricing is way below what it should be. Most people look at Medellín as a place for narcos and violence. That's far from the reality of today's Medellín, as more and more vacationers and expats discover each year.

It's only a matter of time before Medellín's real estate prices rise to reflect the value of what that city is today—a cosmopolitan, First-World city that's seriously on the up.

So How Do You Play a Crisis Opportunity?

There's no magic trick for playing a crisis opportunity. No one way for you to get in at the best moment. The truth is, playing a crisis opportunity well takes time—and patience. Immediately after a crisis is not usually the time to get in. That's not when the best value presents itself. You have to carefully watch the market, assess the economics, and read widely to understand how the market is likely to play out.

In some cases, there will be a trigger event—a moment that triggers the market to bottom out. In the case of Spain and Ireland, that moment was when bank fire sales arrived. That's why I continue to keep a close eye on places like Argentina and Venezuela. I'll be ready if and when a trigger event happens that will make any of the crisis markets I watch a buy.

Even if I see a trigger event, I am very selective when it comes time to make any recommendations. I only recommend the cream of the crop—the real estate that's likely to appreciate strongly as the market recovers. Buying crisis property isn't like shooting fish in a barrel. You need to be thoughtful about what you buy. You should have a picture in mind about how the market is likely to recover—and how the property you buy is likely to perform in that market.

#2: Special Situation Deals—or Personal Crisis Investment

Crisis opportunity doesn't just come from a market that's in crisis. Sometimes, as investors, we can act on what I call "special situation" deals—the chance to buy below market value in a healthy real estate market.

Special situation buys are rarer and harder to find than other types of undervalued property you'll read about in this chapter. They're something you have to keep a close eye out for. Often you'll only hear about one of these special situation buys from a contact on the ground.

When I get word of this kind of special situation buy, the conversation tends to go roughly like this:

"This is a deal like you wouldn't believe, Ronan. But there's only one or two available."

It's not the sort of call I get too often. But I've cultivated a thick black book of real estate contacts around the world who keep me informed. They tip me off when they hear about special situation deals. And when they do, I pay attention. Because often it spells a killer deal.

These special situation deals usually arise when a seller is in personal crisis. They're what I refer to as "distressed sellers"—sellers who need to get out quickly. That could be as a result of divorce proceedings, poor health, or some problems with finances. It's a personal crisis, not a market one. The crisis varies from seller to seller. What remains the same is the fact that the seller wants out—and he is willing to sell under market value to facilitate a quick sale.

Sometimes the opportunity comes out of the blue or on the back of a scouting trip I've taken. The latter happened last year when I traveled to Costa Rica's lake district, Arenal. I was there to scout out an opportunity. I wasn't specifically looking for special situation deals. But when I got word of an unloved guesthouse that could be a nice little earner for an investor with time to spend on a project, I knew I had to see it immediately.

The deal was this: You could own a five-bedroom, three-bathroom guesthouse just a few minutes' walk or bike ride from the town of Nuevo Arenal. The house was in need of serious refurbishment. It needed someone who had the time and will to take on a project. For the right investor, it was a great buy. There's a shortage of rooms to rent short-term in downtown Nuevo Arenal, and this guesthouse could gross you up to $50 a night from each of those five rooms. At full occupancy for just a third of the year, that's a gross of $30,000.

The guesthouse initially listed for $200,000. But the seller had dropped the price to $145,000. He was experiencing some personal issues that made him motivated to sell. I recommended offering $100,000 for it, and spending $30,000 to $50,000 on refurbishment.

This was a complete one-off—the type of opportunity you only hear about from being dialed in to a real estate market and having the contacts who can tip you off about these kinds of deals.

But it's not only individual sellers who offer these special situation deals. From time to time, I also come across developers who want to sell the last unit in a phase of their project so they can focus on the next phase. Or who have a condo that's come back on the market unexpectedly when a buyer falls out. Again, the developers are sometimes willing to cut a good deal to get the property off their books. It's a win-win for them. They get to move their inventory quickly and focus their attention on the next phase of development—and the buyer gets a good deal.

How to Spot Special Situation Deals

As I said, the opportunity to take advantage of one of these special situation buys doesn't happen often. And when one does arise, they're often snapped up quickly. They're usually "blink and you miss 'em" deals.

The easiest way to ensure that you hear about them is to have a strong Rolodex of contacts on the ground who can let you know when one crops up. That's the strategy that works for me. I've spent more than a decade building up those contacts—talking regularly, visiting in person, and maintaining a good relationship. Your contacts can be your most valuable asset when it comes to finding special situation deals on the ground.

You can find these special situations without having that network of contacts on the ground. But it will take more legwork, a lot more time and effort, and a healthy dose of good luck. To do it alone, you'll need to know a real estate market well—including typical pricing within that market. You'll need to know the best neighborhoods and the most up-and-coming ones. And, you'll need to know intimately the market trends that are likely to affect sale prices.

By watching those markets, you may be fortunate enough to spot those one-off opportunities to buy from a distressed seller. A seller who's priced under market value. If you spot one of those opportunities, you could be onto something special. But, as always, you need to do your due diligence to make sure it's the real deal.

#3: Path of Progress Plays

I've spoken to you a little about "Path of Progress" stories already. You'll see the term mentioned in the sections covering the Riviera Maya, Mexico; Northern Nicaragua; and Chiang Mai, Thailand.

The Path of Progress is a term I use often. It's used to describe a very specific event that is influenced by a number of factors. And it can be extremely useful for identifying real estate markets that have the strong prospect of capital appreciation.

A Path of Progress happens when various elements converge to create a market that's set to grow rapidly in the coming years. That sometimes happens because a location is opened up by new infrastructure—roads, airports, or ports.

In other instances, increased investment is due to start flowing into a location. That could be because a new major industry has opened in the area or the local authorities are working to attract tourist dollars. Or government legislation and planning change, so that it's easier than it has been to develop new projects.

Identify a market at the start of a Path of Progress event, and you can do very well on your real estate buy. Get in on the cusp of that major growth trajectory, and your property could increase massively as real estate values rise. (Caveat: You have to make sure that what you buy is what the market wants, even in a Path of Progress event. If you're snapping up family homes when the market wants luxury condos, for example, you'll likely see some capital appreciation—but not as much as you might have if you'd locked down a "hot" luxury condo early on.)

How to Spot a Path of Progress Trend

As with any of these strategies, doing your research will serve you well when it comes to Path of Progress trends.

Every day, I collect information. That information comes from multiple sources. I read news reports, expat blog posts, press releases from government and business people, developers' e-letters, and more. I talk to my contacts, my team, local people, and anyone else who might have relevant information for me. And I watch markets around the world. I look for news of major investments, statistics on growing employment or vacationer numbers, and the rolling out of new projects, like airports and roads.

Once I have a clear "big picture" view of a market, I can spot the factors that might result in a Path of Progress event. You have to be nimble and ready to act when you spot a Path of Progress trend. But, by being well-informed, you're primed to get in first—ahead of other investors who are following the pack, while you're leading it.

CHAPTER 12:

5 Ways to Buy Low to Ensure Maximum Profits

In addition to tapping into one of the trends I spoke to you about in the previous chapter, there are five key ways to buy real estate that could see you maximize your profits from the get-go. Use these to buy property at a price that doesn't reflect its true value, and you could stand to double your investment.

#1: Buying Something Unloved and Adding Value

Sometimes in a healthy market, certain kinds of real estate fall out of fashion. That's not because the real estate has no inherent value. Rather, it's because locals fail to see the value of what's in front of them.

I've seen this happen all over the world. In Latin America, it happens because local buyers tend to favor new builds. So colonial beauties like those I've written about in Nicaragua are allowed to fall into disrepair. It happens in other countries, too. In Ireland, Italy, France, and more, I've seen it happen to the historic farmhouses and cottages that dot the countryside. To an outside buyer, the history and charm that comes with an older home is valuable. To a local, what they see is something "old." But if you're the sort of person who has the time, money, and skills to renovate an older building, you can do very well. Choose right, buy well, and for a relatively small investment, you can grow the value of a historic home.

Take Granada in Nicaragua, for example. There you can profit from an unloved colonial home that's in need of some TLC by restoring it to its former glory.

Restoring a colonial home was a popular strategy in Panama City and Montevideo, Uruguay, in the past couple of decades. Each of these cities has seen a revival of its colonial quarters. Now prices have risen drastically as restored colonials have come back into fashion—especially with foreign buyers.

Granada is quickly rising in popularity with buyers who want a restored colonial. But for now, it's still possible to get in at low pricing.

Granada is Nicaragua's best-known colonial city. And more tourists are coming each year. You can take a day trip to a volcano, on the freshwater lake, or just browse in the boutique shops along the city's main thoroughfare. By night, you can sit on the terrace of a restaurant or bar serving Italian, American, and Nicaraguan fare, and watch street performers.

I've been visiting Granada for more than 12 years. Each time I return, I see how it's growing and gentrifying. That's thanks in large part to the massive focus from the Nicaraguan government on developing its tourism sector over the past decade. Granada is proof of how those efforts have paid off. With every visit I make there, I see its improvement. A new restaurant here, a row of renovated colonials there.

But though its tourist industry has grown, its real estate prices haven't caught up to other Latin American countries.

On one trip in 2013, I found "fixer-upper" colonial homes measuring 2,000 to 2,500 square feet in the historic district for as little as $80,000. More turnkey colonials were going for $160,000. Prices have risen since that trip, but you can still find a colonial bargain in Granada today.

The cheapest ones still go for under $100,000—but they tend to be snapped up quickly. They're getting harder to find as Granada takes off, too. Blink and you'll miss them. They're the ones that need most work. With an added investment of $100,000, you could have a perfectly restored colonial home with a courtyard and perhaps a pool.

Some could be renovated into small hotels or guesthouses. There's a good market here for colonial-style, short-term rentals. When I visited on two separate occasions in January 2016, I struggled to find one to stay in. All the nice rentals I saw were fully booked at $150 a night.

Or you could just own one of these historic homes for your own enjoyment.

Other Unloved Opportunities

It's not just historic properties that get overlooked by local buyers. Sometimes a particular address falls out of fashion. Or a type of property does. So while everyone is buying up three-bed homes, a less fashionable but still comfortable one- or two-bed home might be going for a song. There might be nothing wrong with the address or the property. They might be safe, comfortable, and still close to amenities.

But if no one is buying them, sellers will struggle to offload them. That's where you can pick up a bargain.

(For more on overlooked properties and how you can profit from them, check out the "Auctions" section below.)

#2: Buying at Auction

Buying at auction is very different from buying direct from a broker, seller, or developer. Being in the room and watching in real time as bidders compete can give buyers a rush. But you need to be careful, if you buy at auction, not to let your emotions get the better of you. As with any other way of buying, buying at auction requires research, logic, and a clear strategy. Do it right and you could do well. Buying the right property at auction can lead to a killer deal—a piece of real estate priced well below market value.

I've only touched briefly on auctions in previous chapters. So in this section, I'll go deeper into the opportunity auctions present to you.

How Auctions Work

Auctions are more commonplace in some countries than in others. If you're a U.S. or Canadian reader, you might be more familiar with bank foreclosure auctions.

There are a few different types of auction. They generally fall into these three types: tax- or legal-forced sales; bank foreclosure or bankruptcy; or motivated sellers who need to sell quickly and move on—for all sorts of personal reasons.

An auction typically works like this: A property is put up for sale. The auction house agrees to a reserve price with the seller. The property generally must hit this reserve price or it will be withdrawn from sale. In some cases, the auction house will let it go if it comes in slightly below reserve price, but don't bank on that as a certainty.

Usually, the auction house will give you a description of the property, but often it will not guarantee the description's accuracy. You need to visit the property and do your research before you bid—and you'll need to do due diligence on any property you're interested in before you buy.

Some auctions take place over the course of hours. Others will take place over weeks, giving you more time to examine the property. Some require you (or an agent) to be there in person; some accept phone bids or even online bids. Make sure you're clear on the process before the auction takes place.

When these properties go to auction, they go into a big bargain basket: the kind of bargain basket you'd see in your local department store. If you've ever gone through one of those baskets, you'll know that about 90% of what's in there is junk.

But from time to time, you'll find a true, desirable bargain. Doing your research beforehand will help you distinguish the true bargains from the ones you should leave in the bin.

Here's how I recommend you play it:

- The first thing you need to decide is the play you want to make. In Ireland, that might be buying a vacation home to upgrade and use as a short-term rental.
- Next, pick your location and make a clear decision on how much you're willing to pay.
- Scan upcoming auctions for the type of opportunity that matches your criteria.
- When you find that, put boots on the ground, visit, and have an engineer and lawyer review the opportunity *before* you bid.
- Go into the auction with a clear game plan—how much you're willing to pay, what you want to buy, and what you're planning to do with your property once you've bought.

Here's a run-down of some auctions on my radar right now.

Unloved and Overlooked in Ireland

In 2011, Ireland's auctions were high on my radar. The auction lots came thick and fast—and you could have snagged a killer deal if you chose right.

But these days, the opportunity has slowed down. The country's "bad bank," NAMA, has cleared a lot of the inventory off its books. It doesn't need to sell quite so frequently now. But there's still opportunity to buy well in Ireland. The opportunity now is to buy something unloved or overlooked that local buyers have yet to see the value in.

Ireland's property auctions are mostly run by Allsop (*www.allsopireland.ie*) and Savills (*www.savills.ie/services/residential/residential-auctions.aspx*). They're Ireland's largest real estate auction groups.

In the past year, I've found some killer deals that have come up for auction. They're unloved or underappreciated real estate that local buyers just aren't bidding on. They're missing out on real estate with clear value that smart investors could monetize.

One opportunity that was on my radar in recent months was a vacation cottage in Youghal, a little beachside town about 45 minutes east of Cork City. It's a small three-bedroom home, with only 871 square feet. The second story is under a pitched roof and the property needs an internal upgrade. It was up for auction with a reserve price of €25,000. Even at that price, it wouldn't appeal to many local buyers. I explained to you in Chapter 5 about Ireland's "hated sectors"—the vacation home sector and the rental sector. This little cottage fits into both of these hated sectors. Because of that, the price was low. And local buyers were unlikely to be interested.

But a buyer could do very well on this buy. There's a rental crisis in County Cork now. There's a lot of demand—but not enough real estate to meet that demand. I recently saw a pre-fabricated "studio apartment" advertised for rent. It was 30 minutes outside Cork City, in a very rural area. Make no mistake. This wasn't one of those nice prefabricated houses, made of wood and concrete, that you come across in the U.S. It was a metal container that you often see in Ireland, used as temporary offices on construction sites. Someone had added a toilet with a shower, a small kitchen, and a basic bedroom to this container. Cost of rent for the month—€550.

By comparison, the vacation cottage that's up for auction is almost luxurious. But nobody wants to buy vacation homes. Think outside the box, fix up this unloved vacation home, and you could do well in rentals.

Little Youghal has been overlooked by people who want to buy something to rent out. It's just 20 minutes from pharmaceutical and technology companies in Cork Harbour. But there's a chronic rental shortage in County Cork. You could make a killing by giving this vacation cottage a facelift and renting it by the month short-term to a visiting executive or family that has to relocate short-term.

Another cottage in the same development rents for €300 to €500 a week in peak season. But there's a severe shortage of properties to rent by the month short-term in most of Cork. (As I found when I was looking for a rental for the summer.)

Buy this little home at a really low price, fix it up and make it comfortable with a $20,000 investment, and rent it out. You could rent long-term for €650 a month (subject to your due diligence on whether permitting allows long-term rental). Maybe for €1,200 per month for a short-term rental of two to three months. At 50% short-term occupancy or 100% long-term, that's a potential gross yield of 17% per year. All from an investment of as low as €45,000.

Beware of This Kind of Auction

Back in 2011, I recommended buying family homes in the Dublin 6 neighborhood at auction. Dublin 6 is one of Dublin's more upscale addresses, on the perceived "richer" south side of the city. When I made my recommendation, you could have bought a high-end home in Dublin 6 at auction for $600,000. I said it was a buy. Sellers were struggling to find buyers even for premium properties like these.

Its value has climbed since I made that recommendation... maybe as much as doubled. But things have changed. The real estate market has rebounded. Prices have, too.

There's a lot more competition for auction property in the hottest locations. Five years later, in June 2016, another home, albeit bigger and fancier, came up for auction in Dublin 6. It's close to the location of the $600,000 home I recommended. This house had a reserve of $1.4 million. In just 20 seconds, it exceeded its reserve and the price climbed to $1.8 million. When the hammer dropped minutes later, it had sold for $1.9 million.

That's how auctions play out in a hot market. People bid against each other for the most desirable properties, driving prices higher. That's not the type of auction you should target. You're looking for the other type of auction—where you can buy something unloved, overlooked, or undervalued, where you can profit.

Buying Auction Foreclosures in Italy

As was the case in Ireland, Italy was one of the European countries worst affected by the recession that kicked off in 2008. But Italy's auction story played out differently from Ireland's.

In Ireland there was a property bubble, which included a surge in new construction, followed by a big pop. That's where we got some of our best opportunities to buy at auction in Ireland, as fire-sale auctions cleared the books of NAMA, the bad bank.

Italy was different. The debt was different. It didn't have the oversupply of new builds that Ireland and Spain had. And the banks didn't have the same urgency to clear real estate debt off their books.

The opportunity to profit from auctions in Italy comes mostly from personal debt—especially people who haven't paid the tax man. You can bag a bargain if you buy the right deal at a seizure auction. The government has cracked down on owners who don't pay their taxes. They do rigorous checks to make sure all taxes have been paid. If owners can't (or won't) pay, the revenue service is not shy about seizing their properties.

Again, you need to do your homework. And buy in the right place.

I personally favor locations with a strong vacationer industry, like the Amalfi Coast, or Sicily, or Tuscany. Buy well at auction in any of these locations, and you could do well on short-term rentals.

But you have to know how to find one of these auctions, and what to do to ensure you're getting the best deal. Like a lot of Italian bureaucracy, buying at a seizure auction isn't easy to figure out.

First, you need to research the local real estate market in depth. That will allow you to recognize the true bargains. Do this before you even think of checking out an auction. At auction, you only have a short time to do your due diligence. Don't waste that time doing your research on the local real estate market. You should have that done beforehand.

If you can speak Italian, you'll also be ahead of the game. If not, you'll need to find someone to translate for you. Most listings will not be in English. (Check *www.astagiudiziaria.com/beni_immobili/ricerca/index.htm* for a central listing system of court foreclosures and asset seizures.)

Figure it out and you can find a killer deal.

Let's take, for example, a three-bed condo in a medieval Tuscan town that's just come up for auction. It takes up the first floor of a three-story condo building, has access to its own garage, and a communal courtyard. It has two terraces. It will open for auction at €22,500. The local municipality recommends an extra investment of €5,000 to help it meet modern energy standards, though it says the building is in good condition. I'd wager it could do with an investment of €20,000 to give it a facelift—a total investment of €47,500.

For a similar condo at market rate, you could expect to pay €80,000 or more.

Rare Distressed Buys in Nicaragua

Auctions in Nicaragua are not common. And you aren't likely to find the big bank- or government-run operations you see in Ireland and Italy. Auctions in Northern Nicaragua run where there's a motivated seller and the motivated seller needs to sell within a defined number of days. Then agents put it up for auction.

It's a transparent way of matching a buyer and seller within a short period of time.

Northern Nicaragua is on the up. But it's not yet a fully liquid market. When someone needs to sell quickly, they need to do something to grab attention.

I heard of one of these auctions recently. Only one property was up for grabs. The owner initially had an offer on the property—a 4.5-acre, ocean-view property in a fishing village in Chinandega. On the property is a one-bedroom villa. The owners needed to sell the property quickly. They had some pressing financial obligations to take care of. When the initial offer they had fell through, they decided to auction the property to get a quick sale.

The home listed at $160,000. But by the time it got to auction, the minimum bid price was $115,000. As it happened, two bidders were interested. The winner bid $123,001. That's a savings of almost $37,000 on the original list price.

Auctions Elsewhere in Central America

I've been watching out for other auctions where we can profit in Central and South America—particularly in Panama.

One of my top tips for you if you want to go this route: Get a friend in the bank. Maybe two or three. Make sure they like you. Because that's the only way right now you'll hear about the best deals.

Panama, for example, is known for its discretion. That applies to the bank when it's doing its foreclosures. You could be living next door to a neighbor and talking to them regularly. But your first clue that they've been foreclosed on could well be a removal van turning up.

Even if the bank decides to auction that foreclosed house off, you still might not hear about it.

The best foreclosure deals tend to get offered to the bank's insider contacts. If the property is in good condition, in a good location, and the bank is willing to cut a deal, those properties are quietly bought up and the public likely won't ever hear about them.

So I repeat: If you want to go this route, make sure you have some friends at the bank to clue you in to the best foreclosures before they get snapped up by someone else before auction.

What's left over after the bank's insider contacts have taken their pick is what tends to go to auction. The banks will usually announce these auctions in local newspapers. This is usually property in marginal areas; property that needs a lot of work/renovation; or property that's priced pretty much at market value. There could be a bargain in one that needs renovation—or in an area that's up-and-coming—but you need to do your research and go in with eyes wide open.

Even when a desirable property gets to auction, though, you're not guaranteed a bargain. I have seen a few must-buy auction listings, at least at the reserve price. But on the day, they sold for almost twice the price advertised pre-auction.

Government auctions in Panama are a little more transparent. The government periodically auctions property off that it owns. Examples of this are the "reverted areas" of Clayton, Albrook, Ancón—neighborhoods where the U.S. military/Canal administrators handed back property to Panama's government when they handed back control of the Canal. These properties are auctioned periodically. The properties on offer can be large, generally not for the small investor, though smaller ones do come up from time to time.

The rules are strict. First you have to sign up for the auction. You can do that up to two days before the auction. You must have proof of a deposit (10% or so) in advance to be able to bid on the property you are interested in. This can be cash, a certified check, or a letter from your bank. If you're not successful in your bid, you keep the deposit. Either you or your representative has to be in the room to bid. And you must pay in full for the property within five days. Check *www.areasrevertidas.gob.pa/portal/listadoBienes.aspx* for listings.

For the right deal, the rigmarole may be worth it. But it's not somewhere I see frequent bargains coming up.

Gangsters, Auctions, and Questionable Buys

From time to time, I hear of a property that comes up that sounds like a killer deal at first. But I always look for red flags which indicate that something is not quite what it seems.

The first red flag is the fact that the property tends to be seriously luxurious but priced well below market value. The second is that no local seems interested in bidding.

To an outsider, these can look like a no-brainer deal. Who could let such a good deal pass them by? But there's often a reason these kinds of properties are so cheap—and why a local won't touch them with a bargepole. Remember how the U.S. got Al Capone on tax evasion charges? It's not the only country to have hit on that idea.

In Mexico, tax seizure property auctions come from Hacienda (the country's internal revenue service). In Panama and Italy, the government also runs seizure auctions. That property that looks like a bargain—it could be a *narco's* or a Mafioso's former home. Or in Panama, it could be a Noriega-owned home that the Panamanian government has been trying to sell for years. If that doesn't convince you to do your research before you buy, I don't know what will.

#3: Buying Pre-Construction: Locking in Gains Early

As real estate investors, we make our money buying. That means locking down gains from the get-go. One of the most tried-and-true ways is by buying pre-construction (sometimes referred to as "off plan").

Buying pre-construction has been good to me.

In my early days as an investor, I had success buying pre-construction close to my home patch in Ireland. I bought early-in and saw values soar as my buys were being built.

In all honesty, I got lucky with my timing. I started buying as values soared. I thought I knew what I was doing.

Then I was pitched a deal in a mid-tier city that I was told was vibrant and on the up: more young professionals…more jobs…more buyers and renters. I was offered a lower price than a professional valuation. A bank would offer a mortgage based on this valuation. It was easy—little money down and immediate upside. It all made sense. At least on paper.

The reality, however, was more flat than fizz.

I didn't put boots on the ground before I bought. My visit after buying was an eye-opener. A key part of the idea of buying was the very young and strong population base. But when I visited for the first time, I noticed there were locals working in McDonalds—not immigrant workers, as you'd expect to see in a city with a thriving employment base.

And after taking a walk around the quiet and still sleeping city at 7 a.m., I realized this wasn't the up-and-coming city I'd been sold on, and that the local employment market wasn't as strong as I might have hoped.

Thankfully, it worked out okay. I'm not getting the yield I had hoped for when I bought, but I didn't get burned. But that experience has informed my entire investing career. From that experience, I've developed a clear pre-construction strategy.

There's more that goes into it than just finding an attractive-looking pre-construction project.

Knowing the difference between a good pre-construction deal and a bad one—and what you can do to protect yourself—is essential if you want to do well.

Major Pre-Construction Upside Potential

When you buy pre-construction, you buy based on a set of architectural plans, before a development has been constructed. It's a speculative investment and comes with an inherent—threefold—risk.

First, you're relying on a developer to finish on schedule and deliver what he promised. Second, you're betting on a rising market to keep pushing property prices upward and give you a strong rental demand on completion. Third, you need to factor in your own ability to pay the final lump sum on the property two, three, or even four years down the line.

But with that risk, there's potentially massive upside. Frequently, developers will offer substantial discounts to buy pre-construction. So you can lock in a gain by buying pre-construction. You make a small down payment on something that's often priced below market value. That small down payment gives you leverage.

Done right, this strategy can yield major capital appreciation. And set you up for a strong rental income for life. I've succeeded from it many times in the course of my investment career.

My pre-construction strategy is a two-step idea. You buy for X amount in the early-to-mid stages of a market appreciation cycle; on delivery, as the market appreciates, your property is worth X plus maybe 30% to 50% more than you paid. Then it's set up for a strong rental income (more on rental strategies in Chapter 13). This strategy is at the core of some of my strongest recommendations.

Last year, I took possession of a townhome I purchased in a best-in-class community on Mexico's Riviera Maya. I bought pre-construction when it was being offered to members of my *Real Estate Trend Alert* group at members-only pricing of $215,000. On completion two years later, these townhomes listed for $287,000.

In Northeast Brazil, too, I was able to buy pre-construction condos with low money down—just 1% of the total cost of the condos and low monthly payments along the way. I recently sold one of the beachfront condos I bought for double the price (in local currency). I also banked 18 months' rental income from when I took delivery.

And in Cabo, I locked down a luxury condo, pre-construction, in December 2014, when members of *Real Estate Trend Alert* could get in at members-only pricing of $324,720. Now a similar condo lists in the $450,000 range. I expect my condo to rent for in excess of $46,000 gross a year.

Make Sure the Timing and the Project Are Right

Since my early lesson years ago, I've relied on what sounds like a simple formula for finding my best pre-construction deals: You pick a market that's on the up. Then you find the best opportunity within that locale.

However, identifying a market on the up is just the beginning. The fact that a pre-construction project is in a market on the up is not enough to make it worth recommending. Success depends on a number of factors—including the strength and experience of the developer.

Even in one of the best resorts I've seen, pre-construction success isn't guaranteed. There, more projects have failed than have succeeded. Some never even got off the ground, leaving investors out of pocket for whatever money they had invested.

One developer planned to put in underground parking at his development; he didn't factor in the underground rivers in the area, which ruined that plan and ultimately bankrupted him. One decided to build for a luxury buyer—a buyer like himself. He wasn't thinking of what the market actually wanted, and his development failed because of it.

Even in a promising location, you have to buy from the right developer with the right track record.

A Quick Checklist for Ensuring You're Buying in the Right Location

To do well on pre-construction, you have to choose the right time to buy—in the right location. You need to play the pre-construction market in the early- to mid-growth stages of the market. The market punishes late arrivals who think prices will continue to rise as they have been rising all along.

Buy pre-construction at the top of the market and you risk losing your entire investment. And maybe even more than you have invested, if you are contractually bound to complete and that clause is enforceable. All the benefits of buying pre-construction are tied to a rising and active market. Without a rising and liquid market, pre-construction almost never makes sense.

If there isn't activity in the market, you run the risk that the project you buy into won't be completed... or if it does get completed, half the building will be empty. This can be a big problem when it comes to maintaining communal areas or amenities and security.

But too much interest—at the peak of a boom—can be just as problematic. White-hot pre-construction markets can overheat. Too much supply becomes a problem. Prices rise too fast. If prices rise to the point where there is no expectation of future price increases, the market will stall.

So with all that in mind, the "right deal" should always tick all these boxes:

- An appreciating market in the early-to-mid stages of growth.

- A developer with a strong track record who is financially stable.
- Supply constraints (i.e. there's a factor that will limit new supply). That limit could be lack of land or permitting restrictions. You want to buy in a place where there won't be a flood of supply.
- A market with an abundant supply of end users.
- A liquid market with a large volume of transactions.

If your pre-construction buy doesn't tick all these boxes, it may be time to reconsider.

Know What You're Paying

With pre-construction, you pay a percentage of the property price during construction, typically up to 50%. That allows you to spread payments over the construction period, which can run as long as 36 months. The balance is due when the property is finished.

And some developers in Brazil and Mexico will offer financing on that 50% balance for up to 10 years.

That can be a major advantage where bank financing for foreigners is impossible to get. With pre-construction, it can be easier to get financing in many overseas markets than on completed properties, because you're getting financing direct from the developer. Your financing terms are often better, too.

But you need to agree on the financing terms and conditions with the developer when you buy; don't wait until the property's delivered.

Look out for **adjustment clauses**. Developers often offer lower prices on pre-construction. It works in their favor. They want to keep money coming in during the early stages of their project. At the same time, they want to cover themselves, in case the cost of labor or steel or concrete rises significantly during the construction period. They do that by adding in an adjustment clause to your contract—the highest I've seen is 10% of the purchase price.

An adjustment clause should tie in to official government indices that show a rise in labor costs or raw materials. Your attorney can let you know how to check this.

If there is such a clause, expect that you may end up paying more than the initial purchase price. So, for example, you may initially agree to pay $200,000 for a condo—but when it's delivered, you could end up paying $220,000.

Get What You Pay For

You're buying blind when you buy pre-construction, relying on a glossy brochure and some fancy renders. Unless it's backed up in your contract, you may not get what the salesman promises.

Pre-construction overseas often means "grey finish," so understand before you buy what you'll need to do to make the property move-in ready after the developer hands you the keys. You may need to paint walls yourself, install kitchen cabinetry and shower doors, put in floors or wall tiles, install light fittings, water heaters, or air conditioning units.

You should always ask what specific terms mean. (For example, in Spain, the term "frontline beach" just promises there's nothing between you and the beach—the beach could be a mile away.) As I mentioned in the chapter on due diligence, you can cover yourself by adding highly specific details into your sale contract covering the view you'll get, the finishes, the materials used, etc.

Examining Your Contract

Your **pre-construction** contract is your best chance to protect yourself and your investment—so pay close attention. I always recommend you work with an in-country attorney. Getting the right advice and guidance can save you a lot of stress should any problems happen down the road.

You need to read your contract, too. Often an in-country lawyer may not point out a clause that is usual in his country but that might be different to what you're used to back home.

Check your contract carefully with your in-country attorney to make sure you're clear on what you need to do to **comply** with it. In many countries, if you back out of the sale for any reason after signing your contract, you can be pursued for the entire value of the purchase price. (In Brazil, one of the few exceptions, you get some of your money back.)

Penalties also apply when you're late with a stage payment, or late to close the sale. You usually pay either a flat-rate fine or a percentage of the outstanding balance. But you can make penalties work for you, too. Work with your attorney and you may be able to make them reciprocal.

Also make sure you're covered if the developer is late delivering. I've seen developments completed as much as four years behind schedule, and buyers could do nothing because their contracts didn't state a completion date and didn't include a clause to fine the developer for late delivery.

Finally, think about what happens if you can't **complete the sale** or simply change your mind. If you want to sell fast, you need to ensure you're in a very liquid market. But that's not the only consideration. If you want or need to sell before the property's delivered, you aren't selling a condo, you're **assigning** your sale contract. Some developers allow it and some don't. Those who allow it often ask for a payment (usually a percentage of the price you sell it for or a cut of the profit you make on the sale).

Watch Out for This Pre-Construction Lot Scam

Pre-construction doesn't just apply to condos or homes: You can also buy a lot pre-construction, i.e. before the infrastructure or any amenities have been built. The same inherent risks apply. You're relying on a developer's promise to build roads, put in water and power, maybe build a clubhouse.

There's an additional risk with buying a lot pre-construction, though. A greater risk of fraud or sharp practices. For decades, starting in Florida in the 1960s, disreputable groups have been selling beach or coastal land as an investment. The pitch is that you are land-banking (a concept I'll explain more about below); you buy now and you're promised big appreciation when infrastructure comes later. But, often because of permitting or other issues, the land that's being sold can never be developed—rendering it worthless.

A more recent misrepresentation I've seen is a lot on or near a beach at a super-low price. Thing is, it's pretty much impossible to get permits to build a home here. So, instead of being a cheap beachfront lot, this "opportunity" is actually a complete waste of money.

#4: Land Banking

On to the fourth strategy on our list—land banking. Heard of it before? You might not have. It's certainly not the most fun strategy on our list or the most glamorous. But it's the strategy many of the big boys use. And, done right, it can be one of the most profitable strategies in this chapter.

It's something that I and my team are exploring right now. We've bought a parcel of lake-view land in Arenal in Costa Rica. We're still figuring out the best way to play this land buy. But I expect it to be a big part of Pathfinder's strategy in the future. I'll keep readers of my *Real Estate Trend Alert* abreast of the opportunity as it develops.

It took us a long time to find just the right land-banking opportunity. If it plays out as I expect, it's going to be seriously profitable.

And despite what you might think, you don't need to be wealthy to land bank. Even smaller investors can do this.

So what is land banking, exactly? At its purest definition, land banking is the strategic acquisition of raw land that you hold until an anticipated future event will result in an increase in value. That's a bit of a dry explanation. Think of it as buying in anticipation of a Path of Progress event. You get in before an area takes off—for whatever reason that might be. Do it right and the returns can be huge.

That future event can be one of many. It might be in anticipation of a place taking off with vacationers. (Think Cancún in the 1970s before it took off. Or that beachfront play in Nicaragua I told you about earlier.) It could be farmland. The world will always need food. And, as food becomes scarcer, the best farmland will be worth a lot more. Land bankers who are aware of this have moved in and snapped up good land now—in anticipation of the value that land will have in the future.

Land banking is not a guaranteed strategy. By its nature it is more speculative. You're gambling that the land you buy will appreciate as you expect it to. If your gamble pays off, you could do very well indeed.

So who are the kinds of investors who land bank? They fall into a few different categories.

Speculators

Speculators buy with a plan for a relatively quick flip, based on an expectation that an imminent event is going to dramatically increase demand. A speculator might buy in an area where a new bridge will open up a piece of coast that was previously inaccessible.

Legacy investors

Legacy investors take a much longer view. They're often investing to set their family up for the next generation. They look for somewhere with intrinsic value—beautiful beachfront, for example. The beachfront might be in an area that is currently inaccessible, unfashionable, and completely off the radar. Legacy investors take the view that, given enough time, the perception and accessibility issues will disappear, and they will be holding beautiful beachfront in an area where resort and residential developers will bid prices up.

Developers

Developers always need to have a land pipeline. Remember, the development business is like the mining business. As soon as you start selling lots or condos you are reducing the amount of these you can sell in the future. A real estate development is self-liquidating. Developers always need land in the bank for future projects.

Governments

Governments land bank for nature preservation or to ensure that land is available for future public infrastructure and services.

How to land bank

As I said, this strategy isn't just for the big guys. Individual investors can do it, too. Or if you're comfortable with it, you could join with some friends and/or family to pool your resources. Even an investment of $100,000 could get you in the game.

Here's how you do it.

Pick an area where something that's going to happen in the future will result in an increase in value. Look for infrastructure development—new airports, roads, and bridges.

Try to find a motivated (distressed) seller, someone who needs cash now. Paying less than market value will put you ahead from the get-go.

Don't just choose the cheapest land you see, though. You need to see clear value in your purchase. If it's farmland, make sure that the land is productive and easy to manage.

Or if you're thinking of buying something that will have value for a developer in the future, you need to think like a developer. So you want to ensure that it has some inherent appeal for development. That might include:

- An accessible location.
- Water, electricity, and sanitation close by.
- Easy and transparent permitting process.
- Beachfront.
- Ocean-view.
- Potential for amenities like golf.
- Capacity for high density. The higher the potential density, the more the developer can make per acre, so the more he will be willing to pay for raw land.
- Holding costs. How much will it cost in taxes, security, etc., just to sit on the land?
- Can income be derived from the land while you are sitting on it?

Land banking is not for you if you want to make a quick sale and profit. It's a strategy that hinges on the land's appreciating in value in the long term. If you can't see yourself committing to the purchase for the medium term at least, choose differently. This is not the strategy for you.

But if you're willing to wait it out, land banking may be worth the gamble. Done right, the returns can more than justify the wait and the risks.

#5: Productive (and Valuable) Farmland

"My maid eats yogurt..."

That was how a contact in Brazil explained to me how Brazil was being transformed into a middle-class country. It might sound ridiculous to you: What's the big deal about yogurt? It's something Americans have been eating for decades.

But in some emerging countries, people eating yogurt has traditionally been quite rare. It's seen as a premium product that only the wealthy can afford. The working classes stick to the staples they've been eating for centuries, the same things their parents and grandparents ate.

So when my contact in Brazil told me his maid was eating yogurt, it was a big deal. Yogurt, a premium product of the past, was now something his maid could afford.

I've heard this kind of chatter for years. In Cambodia, Colombia, Mexico, Thailand, Panama, and Nicaragua—right across the globe, poor people are moving into the middle class. And middle-class people have more disposable income to spend. This means they start to consume like we do.

In this book, I've already spoken about how you can profit by owning the home this new middle class wants to live in or rent. But that's not where the opportunity to profit from a growing middle class ends. Look into their refrigerator and another opportunity will leap out at you: the food they consume.

The world is roaring toward food shortages. According to the World Bank, at least 50% more food is needed by 2050 to feed 9 billion people. And it's not just more food that's needed; this fast-growing global middle class wants different foods.

China, for example, has added 100 million new middle-class mouths in the past decade. Brazil has seen its middle class grow by 40 million from 2005 to 2011. Now 54% of the population, or 103 million people, falls within Brazil's middle class.

These trends are so powerful, so unstoppable...that over the medium term they can only push demand in one direction. That means a soaring demand for food. As a real estate investor, my beat is to find and buy cheap real estate and maximize its income, while I wait for big trends to kick in and drive its value up.

Buy right and you position yourself to do very well as the demand for food grows in the coming decades.

What You Need to Know to Buy Farmland

It's not as simple as buying any kind of farmland and waiting for demand to come. Not every farmland deal is a good one. You have to buy right.

Here are the key considerations that you need to make before buying:

- **You need to be able to export and do business in a place where bureaucracy isn't suffocating.** You don't want to do business in a place where a bribe is expected at every step. Or where your product could arrive at the port only to be slapped, seemingly randomly, with an export tariff of as much as 60%. You need to make sure your rights are strong and well enforced.
- **You also need to make sure that the land you own is of sufficient scale that it can work as a stand-alone farm or as a piece of a bigger enterprise.** Farming is a business of scale. The play is to find somewhere with good quality land, availability of water, and good infrastructure, where the government doesn't take a prohibitive cut, and the red tape hassles are few.
- **You want to own the type of land that will be a key input in the global food supply chain.** Then you lease it out and wait for values to skyrocket. Leave the operations of the farmland to the folks who know this game.

Do all this, and choose a productive piece of farmland at the right price, and you have a piece of valuable land in your portfolio that will hold its value and even grow in value as food needs grow.

You don't need to have a farming background to do this. I'm a real estate guy—not a farmer. I don't know how to get crops from a field in Costa Rica to a grocery store in Florida. What I do know is how to figure out mispriced real estate opportunities—and how to find cheap, productive farmland.

My Picks for Where to Buy Farmland

I've told you already about Northern Nicaragua—and how it's on a tear. You could buy a piece of oceanfront land or a colonial fixer-upper here and do very well.

But, if you're in the market for farmland, Northern Nicaragua is still worth your attention. Development land in Northern Nicaragua is cheap today. Not because it isn't productive, but because Northern Nicaragua's real estate market is just getting back on its feet after decades of strife. Prices are still low—this region is still largely undiscovered by outsiders and Nicaragua's out-of-date reputation has depressed the value of land. But the land is fertile, productive. Good, productive land can be bought from $3,000 to $5,000 an acre. And for that you get the kicker of stunning ocean views and future development potential.

Another country to consider is Uruguay. I consider Uruguay the standout locale for foreigners to invest in farmland.

Here's what Uruguay offers:

- **Foreign investors have the same rights as locals.** There are no limitations on the type or amount of land an individual foreigner can buy. Uruguay is a peaceful, democratic country, ranked the least corrupt in the region.
- **Agricultural taxes are low.** Income tax is a flat rate of 25%, but farms with income of less than $238,000 pay a capped tax of only $5,125. Property taxes are also low, at 0.2%, on average.

- **There are no currency controls or exit taxes for money repatriated from Uruguay.**
- **There are no export tariffs.** Neighboring Argentina, for example, taxes many exports. Farmers in Uruguay can stockpile produce and wait for prices to rise, without penalty.
- **The land is mapped and rated with something called a CONEAT ranking so you know how productive it is.** Every piece of land in Uruguay is mapped, checking the soil quality and assigning the land a CONEAT value. That value tells you how productive the land is—and how much it's worth per acre.
- **Uruguay has a temperate climate with year-round rainfall.** It sits on the Guarani aquifer, the largest aquifer in South America. In fact, it's one of the top 20 countries worldwide for water resources per capita. Its soil is also classed as some of the least degraded in the world.
- **Its farming infrastructure is well developed, with service co-ops for harvesting and shipping, a good road network, and trucking services.** Plus, the country already exports to more than 160 countries. And there's a strong farming tradition, with qualified labor available.
- **A ready export market:** There's not much point in raising top-quality cattle or growing amazing grapes for wine if there's no market for it. Uruguay has a strong reputation around the globe for high-quality agricultural produce. It's responsible for 5% of global beef exports. It's the fifth-biggest exporter of dairy products, and the sixth-biggest for soybeans.

Northern Nicaragua and Uruguay are just two countries on my radar for productive farmland buys. You're not restricted to either, but both are a good jumping-off point for comparing the quality of any farmland deals you find elsewhere.

My starting point is to look for excellent farmland with access to water for less than $5,000 per acre. (Prime U.S. and European farmland can cost in the region of $10,000 to $15,000.)

As I said, you don't need to know how to farm to do well with this play. You never have to turn a sod to turn a profit. Instead, rent it out to someone who is in this business.

Don't expect to make a killing on rental incomes (if that's what you're looking for, check out the next chapter, instead). Your yield on farmland will be low. Maybe 2%. But this is a capital appreciation play...a play that will do well in good times and bad. Farmland is the ultimate hedge against inflation.

CHAPTER 13:

Making a Killer Rental Yield

Buying low and selling at a profit is not the only strategy I use to earn from real estate. Making strong rental yields has been a part of my strategy for as long as I've been a real estate investor. Even if you've never considered being a landlord, it's something you should think about.

Many of the most successful investors I know don't just wait for a property to appreciate in value; they rack up impressive rental yields along the way. (Though be advised that it takes time to build up rental income. The payoff, however, can be more than worth it.)

As a real estate investor, having rental income in your portfolio can be one of your most profitable avenues. Done right, a strong rental yield can even help pay for your property. That should never be the primary goal of rental income, though. Think of it as a bonus. If you're not solvent enough to finance the purchase without rental income, you could become one of those distressed buyers I told you about above. Don't let that happen to you.

I've introduced you to a lot of places where you can potentially make a strong rental yield earlier in this book. I won't rehash them here. The places I introduced to you are by no means a definitive list. There are many more worldwide.

Owning what the market wants to rent can give a profitable real estate rental buy.

We'll run through that now. Then you can think about how to maximize your rental yield.

The First 7 Things You Should Do When Choosing a Rental Property

Making the best, most predictable rental yield doesn't just come when you purchase your property. Actually, if you're thinking of buying a property to rent out, you need to do some groundwork before you even buy your property.

There's no point in sinking hundreds of thousands of dollars into a rental property and then discovering you can't legally rent it out—or that the taxes will cripple you financially. They're all things you need to investigate *before* you buy. Here's what you should do before you commit to buying a property to rent out.

1. Check You Can Rent. Get your attorney to check if you can rent out the property you are considering buying. Some countries (Colombia and Panama, for example) restrict short-term rentals in residential buildings in some cities.

If you're buying in a condo building or a private community, check that the bylaws allow you to rent your property out. If you're thinking of renting out a property for commercial use, check that you are legally allowed to rent it out for that use. There may be zoning or permitting restrictions that stand in your way.

2. Buy Low. The price you pay for your home or commercial space determines your rental yield (gross yield is simply the annual rent divided by the property price). You factor in running costs (such as maintenance, monthly fees, and taxes) to get the net yield.

So the less you pay for your property, the higher your rental yield. This is where fire sales and distressed properties come into their own. You'll pay less for these properties than your neighbor, yet you can charge similar rental rates.

Of course, you need to factor in more than the purchase price. Different rental types will have different associated costs.

Compare short-term and long-term rentals, for example. Short-term rentals generate more rental income, but they also carry higher running costs. You'll need to furnish and equip the property. You'll pay for the utilities, cleaning costs, and management fees.

In some markets, you won't need to furnish long-term rentals and the renter covers the cost of utilities. Plus, you'll pay a lower property management fee for a long-term rental. That bumps up your yield.

3. Buy the Right Unit. It's always important to buy in the right location. With a rental investment, you need to buy the right property in the right location for your target market.

In cities, you'll find that certain locations appeal most to short-term renters. They're usually spots where you don't need a car to get around, close to financial districts, shopping, entertainment, and night-life. You'll maximize your profit in these locations by purchasing a one- or two-bed condo and renting to tourists or business executives.

I've met folks who generate a healthy profit from small studios in downtown locations. But a cramped studio or a tiny one-bed condo won't work in a neighborhood that only appeals to long-term renters and families.

Buyers often get carried away and purchase a luxury, ocean-view penthouse. It won't generate a decent yield if there's no demand for that type of unit, though.

To get a good overview of the local market—and what type of units are in hot demand and generate the most income—speak with as many real estate agents and property management companies as possible. You can also check out the classified section in newspapers, online rental sites, and ask locals that you meet.

4. Investigate Occupancy Levels. Don't rely on tourist numbers to figure out your occupancy rate. Tourist numbers include locals returning home, cruise ship passengers, and people visiting friends. They will never rent a property but they can make up a big chunk of tourist numbers.

Hotel occupancy rates give you a better handle on the market. But don't rely on occupancy rates to stay high. Panama City achieved a record hotel occupancy rate of 84.7% in 2007. Today, occupancy in the city hovers around 50%. That's due to a large increase in the number of new hotel rooms. We'll explore that more in the next tip.

5. Check the Competition. You need a market with strong demand for your type of property and ideally little competition. For short-term rentals, that means a lack of decent, affordable hotel rooms and short-term rental condos. For long-term rentals you should look for areas with a shortage of rental condos or houses or a gap in the market. You may find a demand for three-bed houses close to a good school or a shortage of office space in a city with a growing economy.

Check the current number of hotel rooms and rental units in the market and check supply in the pipeline. In a slow market, where owners can't sell, many switch to renting. If that slow market has thousands of condos due for completion and thousands of hotel beds in the pipeline, your rental yield will suffer.

6. Look for Spots With All-Round Appeal. Widening your market of potential renters will keep your rental yield high. Locations that attract a combination of tourists and business travelers, or domestic and foreign tourists, will keep your property full and your yields strong.

If you're renting short term, look for places with year-round appeal. It's harder to make a decent profit if your high season only lasts for two months. For long-term rental, look for areas where a growing economy and business opportunities bring in executives and professionals for longer periods.

7. Get the Lowdown on Taxes. Investigate your tax liabilities. Tax on rental income varies widely. You'll pay 0% in some Caribbean tax havens, up to 30% in Costa Rica. Find out if you can offset expenses against that tax, look up local property tax rates, and ask if there are any other taxes (wealth tax, luxury tax, school tax) that apply to your property.

If you plan on sending the rental income back to your home country, ask if you'll have to pay any extra taxes for wiring money outside the country. Remember, you may still have tax obligations in your home country.

How to Maximize Your Rental Yield

Once you've bought your property, you need to think about your strategy to maximize your potential yield.

As discussed, you'll be well served if you find a destination with year-round appeal—whether that's from long- or short-term renters. Personally, I seek out destinations where a Path of Progress event is about to happen or is currently underway, such as a new airport that will bring more people: destinations where you can tap into an existing or growing rental market with money to spend on the right property.

But doing well on a rental property is not as easy as buying a nice place and hoping renters will show up. If you're asking renters to part with their hard-earned cash for your property over a competitor's, you need to be sure that what you're offering beats the competition. Your rental property is a product. And you need to treat it like one.

It's competitive out there. Winner takes all. Identifying the right destination to earn a strong rental income is an important part of the equation, but it's not the only one. It's the first step. The next step is to maximize your return.

Approach your rental strategy in the wrong way, and you'll leave money on the table…or worse, push people to the competition. Little things can make a big difference in how your rental property performs. Follow these simple, tried-and-tested steps, and you stand to double or even triple your rental yield.

Give Yourself Time to Build Your Income

Creating a portfolio of income-generating properties is something I believe strongly in as a real estate investor. Creating such a portfolio is part of my own personal strategy. I'm setting up my buys in Cabo and the Riviera Maya in Mexico to create an income stream. When I retire and no longer have an income from work, those real estate buys will be generating a strong rental yield.

I don't expect to be earning big right out of the gate. I understand that it takes time to get an income-generating portfolio to maximum potential. Don't rely on that income to cover your costs, at least not in the early stages.

Take a medium-term approach to building income. It will take work to get there. As with any other real estate investment, you have to have a strategy in mind as to how you will make money from your rental property. That largely comes down to how you market your property.

Advertise Right and Get Noticed!

I can't begin to tell you how many good rental properties go overlooked because the owner hasn't advertised it properly.

Say you've got a luxury condo that's a few steps from a beautiful beach and a stroll to a gourmet restaurant. It's in a community with top-notch amenities and amazing views. How well do you think it would rent if you use a photo of an overgrown field to advertise it?

That's not a hypothetical question. Believe it or not, this is what I found when I booked a rental condo online recently. I was scouting and needed a place at short notice. I fully expected to pay a high price for my stay. I knew the community I wanted to stay in. It was high season and I didn't think I'd find anything available to rent. But one condo had slipped through the net—because its owner is doing such a terrible job promoting it.

Because I knew the area well, I was happy to take a chance on renting her property. I know the community and even the condo block her property is located in well, so I knew for a fact that I'd have at least a comfortable stay in a good location. Other prospective renters likely would not. Based on the photo she had chosen to promote her luxury condo, I guessed most renters would be unwilling to take a chance on renting the property, either short- or long-term.

On arrival, I met the owner. My assessment was right. She couldn't understand why her condo wasn't renting as well as others in the community. I shared some tips with her.

Advertise in the Right Places

If you're planning on renting short term, I recommend you use an established vacation rental-by-owner website that's high profile, an established brand. There are several of these: VRBO, FlipKey, and Airbnb are among the most established.

If you plan to rent your property longer term, you should check out the most established websites for long-term rentals in your particular destination. And work with local real estate agents and property management companies.

If you use an agent or management company to find a tenant for a long-term residential rental or a commercial unit, they will usually take a one-off advertising fee equivalent to one month's rent on a 12-month contract.

Generally, short-term rental sites take a percentage of what you charge your renters as payment for using their service. That's a fee you wouldn't pay if you were to advertise on your own personal website. But there are advantages to using these services that make it worthwhile for a lot of vacation rental owners.

The biggest advantage to sites like these is visibility for your rental property. The big names in the business spend a lot of time and money making sure they come out on top when someone searches online for rental property. That means more traffic on their site—and more potential renters for your property. In turn, it means you won't have to fight to have your property seen by online searchers.

The well-known brands are trusted by renters, too. That's another advantage to using them. Some of them operate a full-refund policy to renters if things go wrong. That helps potential renters feel more secure. It also pushes them from simply browsing to making a booking.

If you're going it alone to advertise your short-term rental, get a professional to help with your website. It should look appealing, well laid out and easy to navigate.

Whether you're using a brand-name site like this or managing your own website, renters should get an easy one-step booking and payment process. Most folks are time pressured these days. The quicker and easier the booking process, the better. Bigger sites allow renters to book and pay on the spot using a credit card.

As an owner, you should explain your cancellation policy clearly, and make it available to renters before they book or pay. You should also give renters a copy of your rental rules.

A Note on Using Services Like Airbnb, FlipKey, and Others

Not everyone is as big a fan of short-term property rentals as investors are.

Some cities with housing crises, particularly in Europe, are banning short-term rentals. Berlin is one of the most high-profile cities to restrict them. The law doesn't apply to rooms rented in private homes while the owners are there. What it does prevent is renting entire premises to tourists.

> Authorities took the step in light of a severe shortage of long-term rentals in the city. It had an immediate effect. Listings on Airbnb for Berlin fell by almost 40% in just one month. Owners had a good incentive to delist their properties: If you were found to be in breach of the rules, you could face fines of up to €100,000. So it made sense to comply.
>
> Not everywhere has rules like Berlin. Many growing tourism destinations are welcoming short-term rentals, as they help to grow visitor numbers.
>
> But if you're considering renting out your entire property to vacationers, you need to know the rules and obligations of your chosen destination.

Deliver More Than Your Competition at the Right Price

Researching the competition is key to making sure you stand out. Look at your competition to make sure your pricing is right. See what they're doing—and make sure you're matching (if not beating) that.

Let's take short-term rentals as an example. Say you're renting at $150 a night, and so is your neighbor. But your neighbor's identical home is kitted out with A/C, a washer/dryer, and free WiFi, and yours isn't. In that case, you'll either have to match those amenities or cut your rate.

Or if you're planning on renting long term or a commercial property, think about what your renter wants. If your long-term residential property is close to public transport and amenities, use that as a selling point to potential renters. If you're renting out office space, and all of your competitors offer air-conditioning as standard, then you should, too.

Lastly, customer service is key. If you're advertising your property yourself (rather than using an agency or a management service), follow up with potential renters as quickly as possible. If they email, respond promptly and give them all the details they need. Give your phone number and let them know they can call you if they have any further questions.

Tips for Advertising Your Short-Term Rental Property

- A picture is worth a thousand words. Choosing the wrong photos can actually put off prospective renters.

  Your home is only as good as the photos you show of it. Get some help taking the photos if you need it...and use your best photo as your "profile" photo. It's the first thing folks will see when they search.

  Bad lighting, weird camera angles, and photos of dark corners won't help. Make sure your home looks its best. Stage it as if you're selling it to a prospective buyer. Declutter it and remove any personal items you've scattered around. Make it look warm and inviting. If you've got outside entertaining space, show it off. If you're close to a beach, post some nice beach shots.

- Come up with a catchy one-line title that makes your home stand out ("Luxury Condo by the Beach and Close to 5-Star Restaurants," for example). It should sound compelling enough to make people want to click on it and find out more.

- You'll also need a good description of your home. Bigger vacation-rental-by-owner sites will give tips on what's expected as standard in a property, down to the number and type of towels in each bathroom.

  List what rooms you have and what furniture and appliances you've got, down to the type of bed and how many place settings you're offering. Describe the area around your home—the amenities and attractions nearby. State how close they are to your home. Mention a few good places to eat and shop; give the names of the eateries and the type of food they serve. Most importantly, paint a picture of the dreamy vacation your guests can enjoy.

A word of caution, though. Deliver what you promise. If you describe your home as "luxury," renters will expect fine linens, top-notch furniture, and quality finishes. Don't tick to say you've got a beach view if you haven't...or that your home is a "few steps" to town when it's a half-hour hike. You'll just get unhappy renters and bad reviews.

- With many online vacation rental sites, you'll have access to a calendar that you can program to show when your property is available. Updating your calendar regularly is a must. Some sites will automatically update it every time you get a booking. But if you don't get a booking, manually update it. Some sites partially de-list properties with outdated calendars so that they don't show at all if a renter is searching for availability on specific dates.
- Think about what your renters want. A little tactical thinking will go a long way. A contact who has properties in Medellín, Colombia, told me he's fitted all his rental properties with air-conditioning—even though the climate is so temperate air-conditioning is rarely needed. His reasoning? Most North American renters will automatically tick "air-conditioning" when searching for a place, even when it's not needed. By including that one amenity, he ensures he's visible to a bigger pool of renters than his competitors who don't offer air-conditioning.
- Keep an eye on peak seasons and events to get the best price for your place. Adjust your rate seasonally—or

to reflect local events such as film or jazz festivals, when demand is higher. You may want to set a minimum stay period in peak season, or to fit with local short-term rental restrictions.

- The currency you charge in is important. If most of your overhead is in dollars, it seems obvious to post a nightly or weekly rate in dollars. But if your potential renters are mostly local, and dollars aren't widely available, it's another hurdle that potential renters may not want to cross.
- Finally, get reviews (preferably good ones!). Many folks won't rent a property if it doesn't already have reviews. If your renters enjoy their stay in your home, they usually won't mind posting a review to your site. You can always encourage them to post a review by giving them a discount off their next stay if they do so.

Using a Property Manager Versus Going It Alone

Whether you use a property manager or not is completely up to you. You should weigh up how much time you feasibly have to devote to managing, promoting, and maintaining your property. Dealing with tenants can be a time-consuming process.

On the other hand, if you have the time to spare, it may be worth it to forego a property manager to save the money you would pay one.

If you decide a property manager is the right course of action for you, it can be a lucrative move. A good property manager can make all the difference between an average rental yield and a great rental yield. And if you're looking for a hands-off rental property, you'll need a property manager that covers all the bases. A manager should find tenants, check them in and out, pay utilities, and deal with plumbing emergencies at 3 a.m.

Ask for their rates in writing. For short-term, you'll pay anything from 15% to 40% of the rental income in fees. Some companies charge a fixed rate per month (which you'll pay even if you don't have renters). That may be worth it if they have a good track record. If they don't, you'll be throwing money away.

For long-term management, you'll pay 50% to 100% of the first month's rent if they find you a tenant, and then a low monthly charge of 5% to 15% if you want them to take care of maintenance, repairs, bills, and any issues the renter has. Make sure that you're clear on what the management fee covers.

Ask how many units your manager currently handles. Find out what systems they have for handling reservations, queries, and reporting problems. Check if it is an established company with a large client base or a start-up with no track record.

An established company should give you a clear idea of how much rent you're likely to get and how much profit that translates to. Check the data the company provides with other sources. Ask for referrals from clients, too.

Get your attorney to draw up a standard rental contract and make sure that your property manager uses it with every tenant.

CHAPTER 14:

When to Make Your Exit

At this point you're well versed in how to buy low. And how to make killer rental yields. But that's not the end of the story. You need to know the right time to sell your property.

Buying—and selling—well should be exciting, fun at times, and your path to profit. The advice that follows is all about ensuring that's how your purchase plays out. I'm giving you this advice because I want to make sure you buy what's right for you—and that it proves to be a profitable and pleasurable experience.

You need to assess both yourself and your purchase. By doing that, you take emotion out of the equation. And you start to look at your investment from a businessperson's perspective—not from a personal one.

You need a strong and clear exit strategy. It's essential if you want to benefit from strong capital appreciation and/or strong rental yields.

An exit strategy means knowing how you're going to exit your real estate investment…understanding who your buyer or renter is going to be…and if he can pay the price you want to get a good return.

How Do You Know What the Right Exit Strategy Is?

Your personal, financial, and investment circumstances will shape your exit strategy. You and I could make exactly the same investments, yet our exit strategies might be completely different.

Let's say you need funds for retirement in 10 years. This needs to be figured into your exit strategy, which feeds into the opportunities you then decide to act on. You won't be interested in a play that's buy and hold for 15 years. You want your money sooner.

Everyone has different requirements for their money or for accessing their cash. And some people just have different attitudes on how to invest. Some people want to lock down an investment long term; others like to play with their investments. Most *Real Estate Trend Alert* readers are investing for retirement or to have funds available at a later date. This feeds into their personal exit strategy, as it will determine when they need to exit.

Before I go into any detail on exit strategies, there's something I'd like to stress: At the heart of the plays I invest in and the recommendations I make, you need to figure on buying and holding. I don't play the quick-flip angle.

The key to doing well with buy and hold plays is to be a flexible investor. To be flexible, you have to be well funded—not in a position where you need to sell at short notice. My top recommendation as the foundation for any exit strategy is: Be in a position to hold for the foreseeable future.

You need to be able to sell at the right point in time. When you're ready, there needs to be someone on the other side who is willing to buy when the investment runs its course, and rent as you go. From the get-go, you need to have that exit strategy in mind.

To figure out your exit strategy, you need to understand how smart real estate investing works.

How Market Liquidity Works for You

Buying and selling real estate is nothing like trading a stock in Apple or GM. Except in a catastrophic moment, those stocks will always have a price—a clear and transparent ticker price. You can just call up your broker, issue a sell order, and have it executed in minutes. This is an example of a liquid market.

But the real estate markets I recommend fall along a liquidity spectrum. "Liquidity" refers to how fluid a real estate market is. A liquid market is one in which there are plenty of buyers, fast sales, and the asking price for property is usually met or even exceeded. An illiquid market is one in which real estate sales are slow or stalled, a market in which you will have to cut your selling price in order to move your property.

The liquidity of a market can move over time. And each end of the spectrum offers different benefits to smart real estate investors. Illiquidity is your friend when it comes to buying. Lack of liquidity on the seller's side can create those special situation opportunities I told you about in this book. The seller needs cash in a hurry. So you get a killer deal.

Where an illiquid market will hurt you is if you're the one who's in a distressed situation. You never want to sell at a point when you're backed into a corner and have to get out quickly. Do that and you'll likely lose money on your investment. Instead, you need to be able to sit on your property investment and sell when the moment is right.

The strategy is to buy low. Then to sit back and hold the property in whatever the appropriate way is—whether that's generating rental income or just keeping raw land safe. The smart move is to exit when the moment is right and the market strong—when the buyer is lined up, not when cash is short and you need to make a quick sale.

That's why an exit strategy is so important. It allows you to exit when the time is right, not when your back is against the wall.

Why You Need to Be Sure You're Well-Funded Before You Buy

Part of a good exit strategy is managing your finances. This is where being totally honest with yourself is important. You may like the idea of a certain deal. But if you're not certain you can pay for it with your own money, back away.

That's why I cautioned you in Chapter 13 never to rely on rental income to pay for your purchase. It's also why you should be sure you can make all payments that are expected of you if you're buying pre-construction.

I like the leverage I can get with pre-construction. When done right, it puts a buyer ahead from the beginning.

But when it comes to funding, I'm always ready to go the whole way with a property. I ensure that I'm well-funded enough to be able to carry the cost of my purchase until it is paid off. I calculate whether I can make all the necessary investments and repayments by myself, as if the property will never make me a penny—even if I'm planning on targeting rental income.

You need to be realistic about the costs. Say a particular deal requires you to make stage payments of 50% during construction and a one-off payment of the balance of 50% due on delivery. You're offered financing by the seller. That's a nice bonus if you're well-funded.

But if you're unlikely to be able to pay that final 50% on closing, and the financing you were promised doesn't pan out, that puts you in a vulnerable position. You may have to sell quickly and take whatever you can for the property. You may lose the property if you can't come up with the closing balance. You do not want to be in that position.

When you're offered financing by a seller or developer, you should always get a watertight contract that spells out the financing deal before you commit to buying the property.

I am conservative by nature, and because of the liquidity of real estate markets and the costs of buying and selling, everything I buy or recommend is a minimum three- to five-year hold. (There can be exceptions when a market moves crazy-fast in the right direction and when you can exit earlier, but that is the exception, not the rule.)

But when playing some deals, you need to think of them in the longer term, too. You need to be ready and comfortable to hold out beyond three to five years. That's especially true when it comes to land banking.

Even if you're holding for the medium term, you need to ensure you exit at the right time. That means having the funds to see a project through to completion, particularly when it comes to pre-construction deals. You don't want to have to exit a project when it's still a building site. You won't have end-users lining up to buy at that point. Your earliest exit moment is when the community is fully established and buzzing. That's when you stand to make a profit.

When planning your exit strategy, make sure you are always in a position to buy and hold until you can at least recoup your investment.

Have Your Eventual Buyer in Mind From the Start

A smart exit strategy will always take into account who your buyer is. What you buy should be determined by who that is. If you plan to sell to the local market, you'll want to buy a property a local will want to own. And in some cases, what a local wants is not the same as what you want.

In somewhere like Brazil, you're buying with a view to selling to the local market. In the case of Spain, you're buying distressed with a view to ultimately selling to a Northern European; in the Riviera Maya your market is North American.

With any deal, you always need to have in mind to whom you will sell and whether or not they'll have the funds to buy.

Take the situation in Medellín as an example of a market where you know to whom you will sell. I predict the larger condos are the ones Medellín's upper middle class will want to own. Part of my recommendation is to hold for five to seven years.

These condos are dated. But another part of my recommendation is not to do anything to update them right away. Why? Because when you sell in five to seven years, your buyer will either want something new and shiny—or a blank canvas they can update to their tastes.

Market tastes and styles change over time. Update one of those condos now and it will be outdated again when it comes time to sell. It's a waste of your time and money to update it as soon as you buy it.

If selling to the local market, you also need to be aware of what they don't want—the anomalies of the local market. In Brazil, for example, if you're selling to the local market, you'll want to buy a home that faces east. That's different from, say, Spain, where buyers will want something facing west or south. That's because Brazilians don't want strong afternoon sunshine; it means more air conditioning use, which racks up electricity costs (which are generally higher in Latin America).

Understanding who your eventual buyer is a key component of a good exit strategy.

Sometimes Your Strategy Will Change

This isn't all written in stone. In actuality, you should be prepared for the fact that your strategy might change.

When you have your exit strategy figured out from the start, you put yourself in a strong position. But sometimes you may need to adjust. That's the nature of real estate buying.

A good example of this is Northeast Brazil. I've been bullish on this area for several years—and I've done well from it.

In any market, things bounce around—currencies, for example. That's not a problem for me because I'm following a carefully-planned strategy. I'm not worried by the drop in value of Brazil's currency, the *real*. Currencies fluctuate; you need to roll with changes in currency. What happens to the currency is a medium-term blip.

But something *did* happen in Brazil that made me readjust my initial exit strategy.

When I first purchased in Brazil back in 2008, my plan was to buy pre-construction condos with a low down payment (1%) and monthly payments of 1% during the build period. I bought in prime areas, from established developers, in projects with a minimum three-year build period. The condos I bought offered the prospect of strong capital appreciation.

My exit strategy was to accumulate a portfolio of income-generating rental properties. I expected to sell some properties along the way to help fund other purchases or to pay outstanding debt on the condos I purchased. However, at no point would I have to sell to make stage payments on my properties. I had a cushion at all times.

But, as I said, my exit strategy changed over time. This had nothing to do with the political problems in Brazil or the decline in the value of the *real*. Some of the cash I freed up I re-invested in Brazil. I decided to sell because I felt that, over the next three to five years, I can do better from capital appreciation from raw land rather than renting out my condos. I can make more money from other investments.

Buying and Renting

Many of the deals I bring to *Real Estate Trend Alert* members have a strong rental kicker. That's a key part of my personal strategy: to create a portfolio of income-earning properties.

For example, with my purchases on Mexico's Riviera Maya and in Cabo, my idea is to create a portfolio of properties. I cover the stage payments during construction. From delivery, I expect the rental income to come close to covering finance costs. (But I'm not relying on the rental income to cover the financing, and neither should you.) The financing is typically over five years. Then I'm free and clear, with positive cash flow.

I'm setting up these real estate buys to create income, even though I don't need the income right now. I'm setting myself up for the future, when I don't have an income. The reason I'm doing it now is that it can take a long time to build up an income-generating portfolio.

Selling Your Property

Of course, the end result of any exit strategy is selling your property for a profit—and that's something you'll need to consider carefully to get the best return on your investment.

When you think it's time to sell, there are some things to keep in mind to maximize your potential profit.

The first thing to do is to check out your competition. That might be a homeowner or a developer. Look at true comps. If a developer is offering the same home as yours, brand-new, with low-cost developer financing, you can't expect to match his current list price and sell. You need to be competitive and realistic.

Let's say you buy for $100,000 and, five years later, everything is going gangbusters, and the developer is selling for $200,000 but he's offering financing. In that case, you should price your property at $180,000 to be more competitive.

When it comes time to sell, getting creative can help to bump up your profit margin. You might want to consider getting paid in installments, for example, if you're selling to a North American in a market where foreigners can't get a bank loan.

When considering any real estate opportunity, having an exit strategy in mind is an integral part of the investment. You need to have a clear idea of your planned exit strategy when you're buying.

AFTERWORD

Everything you've read about in this book comes from many years of experience—and these are all tactics and strategies I'll continue to use in 2017 and beyond.

This year, my travel schedule is packed full. I'll be traveling to dozens of destinations that I see as having big real estate potential. That's how confident I am about the opportunity to profit on the right buy overseas—I'm racking up air miles and wearing down shoe leather to dig deeper into the opportunities out there today.

Let me tell you that 2017, plain and simple, is *the* year for overseas real estate investment. That's not something I say lightly: That assessment is based on my years of experience and what I'm seeing on the ground right now. Everything is lining up to make 2017 a banner year for buying property overseas.

The dollar is close to all-time highs—especially against several of the local currencies in some of the locations with the most real estate upside potential on my beat. That means your buying power stretches further overseas as I write this: particularly in markets with the peso (in Mexico), the real (Brazil) and the euro. You can lock down more, in a place that's set for big capital appreciation, for less money.

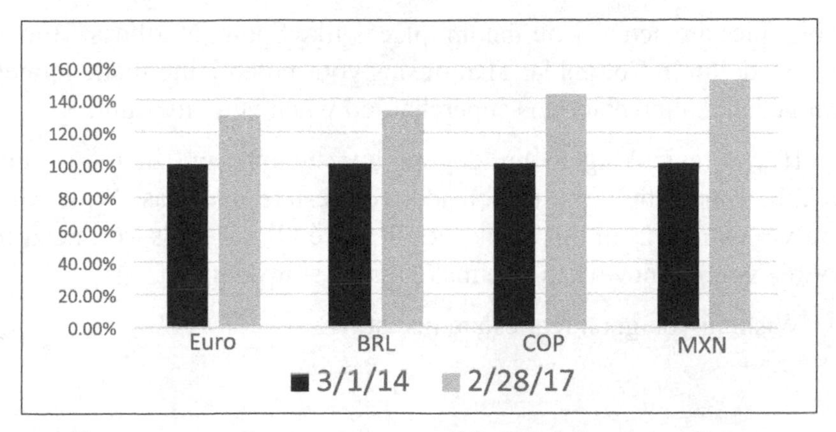

The increase in value, in percentages, of the U.S. dollar against the euro, Brazilian real (BRL), the Colombian peso (COP), and the Mexican peso (MXN) between 1 March 2014 and 28 February 2017.

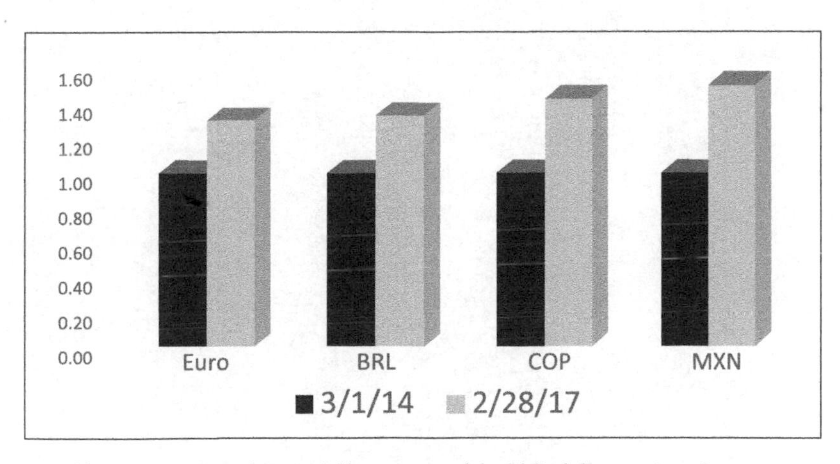

The increase in value, in dollar terms, of the U.S. dollar against the euro, Brazilian real (BRL), the Colombian peso (COP), and the Mexican peso (MXN) between 1 March 2014 and 28 February 2017.

If you know where and how to invest, as I've discussed in this book, you'll be on track to identify some great opportunities to lock down real estate at crisis or undervalued pricing—in places whose economies are actually on the up: places like Spain, Northeast Brazil, and Medellín in Colombia. That means your potential to make money from capital appreciation is supercharged when you buy right.

If you're looking to build your investments and increase your wealth, *now* is the time to consider real estate overseas. With what you've learned from this book, you'll have all the tools you need to double your money when you make that first investment.

Wishing you good real estate investing.